W9-CMU-572

exploring the weather

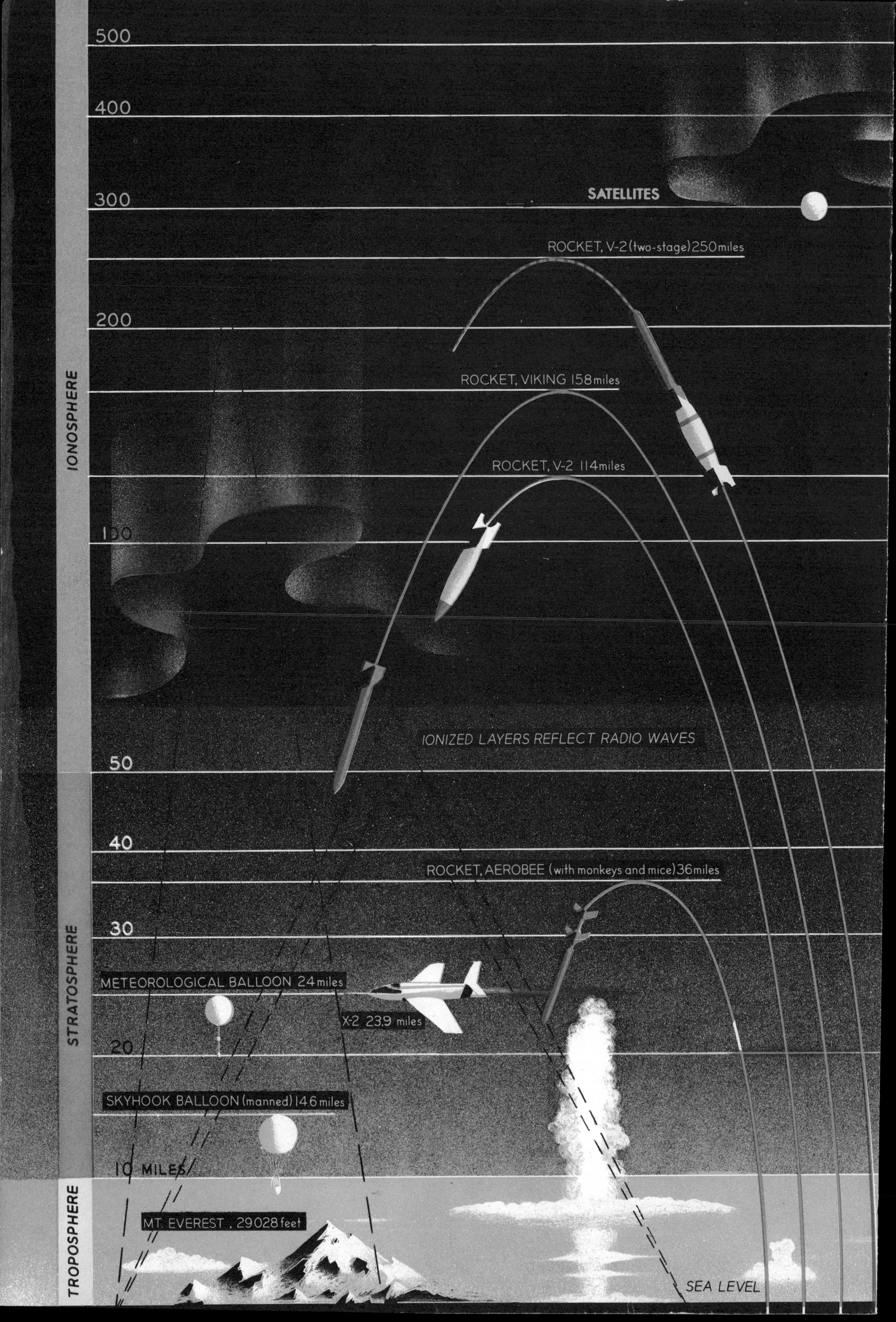
500
400
300
SATELLITES
ROCKET, V-2 (two-stage) 250 miles
200
ROCKET, VIKING 158 miles
ROCKET, V-2 114 miles
100
IONIZED LAYERS REFLECT RADIO WAVES
50
40
ROCKET, AEROBEE (with monkeys and mice) 36 miles
30
METEOROLOGICAL BALLOON 24 miles
X-2 23.9 miles
20
SKYHOOK BALLOON (manned) 14.6 miles
10 MILES
MT. EVEREST, 29028 feet
SEA LEVEL
IONOSPHERE
STRATOSPHERE
TROPOSPHERE

exploring

the weather

BY ROY A. GALLANT
ILLUSTRATED BY LOWELL HESS

GARDEN CITY BOOKS, GARDEN CITY, NEW YORK

FOR LARRY, JR.

A sailor must know his weather

SCIENCE BOOKS BY ROY A. GALLANT

EXPLORING MARS
EXPLORING THE MOON
EXPLORING THE UNIVERSE
EXPLORING THE SUN
EXPLORING THE PLANETS
EXPLORING CHEMISTRY
EXPLORING THE WEATHER
MAN'S REACH INTO SPACE

The author's thanks to Ernest J. Christie, U. S. Weather Bureau, New York City, for his helpful suggestions regarding the manuscript of this book and to Duell, Sloan & Pearce, Inc., for permission to adapt The Insect Thermometer on page 9 from an illustration in Eric Sloane's *Weather Book*, Copyright 1949-52 by Eric Sloane.

LIBRARY OF CONGRESS CATALOG CARD NUMBER 57-6175

PRINTED IN THE UNITED STATES OF AMERICA

contents

S
W
E
N

what is weather?

Mostly sunny this afternoon with temperatures well up in the seventies.
Fair and cool tonight. Lowest around sixty.
Tomorrow mostly fair with increasing cloudiness late in the day. . . .

This is a typical weather picture which any of us can read in our newspaper. Or we can hear it simply by flicking the dial of our radio or television set at the right moment. New Yorkers are luckier than most people in the country. They don't even have to wait for the "right moment." Any time of day or night all they have to do to hear the latest weather forecast is pick up the telephone and dial WEather 6–1212. A girl's voice on tape recites the latest weather news like the forecast above. According to the Weather Bureau, the mechanical weather girl repeats her message to more than 50,000 New Yorkers who dial her number every day. The record number of calls in one day is 374,781! If there were some way of listening in on every conversation in the world—at this very moment—you would probably find the weather leading all topics.

When the weatherman's forecast for tomorrow turns out the way he said it would, we admire him. In a sense he has predicted the future for us, and in a way no fortuneteller would ever dare try. He not only tells us that it will be fair, but he tells us what the temperature will be within five degrees. What fortuneteller would risk her "reputation" by giving us such pointed information? Usually fortunetellers make their predictions safe by being vague. For example, one of them may tell you, "Soon you may expect good news." "Soon" can mean tomorrow, next week, or next month. And "good news" can mean a note from Aunt Susy saying that she is sending the five dollars she promised you, or it can mean the "A" your arithmetic teacher gave you. When the fortuneteller gives you information, what she means is anyone's guess. But when the weatherman gives you information, there can be no mistake about what he means.

In a way the weatherman is like an architect, or housebuilder. The architect has certain materials to work with—lumber, concrete, glass, bricks, and metal. Depending on how he plans to put these materials together, he can show you a picture of the house he intends to build for you. The weatherman also has "materials" to work with. They are huge parcels of air hundreds of miles wide which sweep down on us from Canada and flow across the country. They are "fronts," caused when a warm air mass collides with a cold air mass. They are clouds, heat of the land and water, and many other things. Depending on how nature arranges the weatherman's materials, he can show you a picture of tomorrow's or next week's weather.

Meteorology, which is the formal name for the study of weather, is one of the newest sciences. Compared with chemistry and physics meteorology is still an infant. Because it is so new we find few weather-wise men in ancient times.

About 2400 years ago the Greek philosopher Socrates made an amusing comment which shows that he knew something of the weather's behavior. His comment describes his wife, Xanthippe, who often flew into rages and flung dishes at poor Socrates. When he later told his friends about these attacks he would sigh and say, "I should have known that when Xanthippe began to thunder, it would soon rain."

It isn't until recent times, not much more than two centuries ago, that we find weather "sayings." These sayings show that some men carefully observed the weather and came to realize that certain signs usually meant that a special kind of weather was brewing. Several of these sayings have been collected by David Bowen, a British writer who specializes in the weather. Here are some of them:

A good hearing day is a sign of wet. Today's meteorologists know

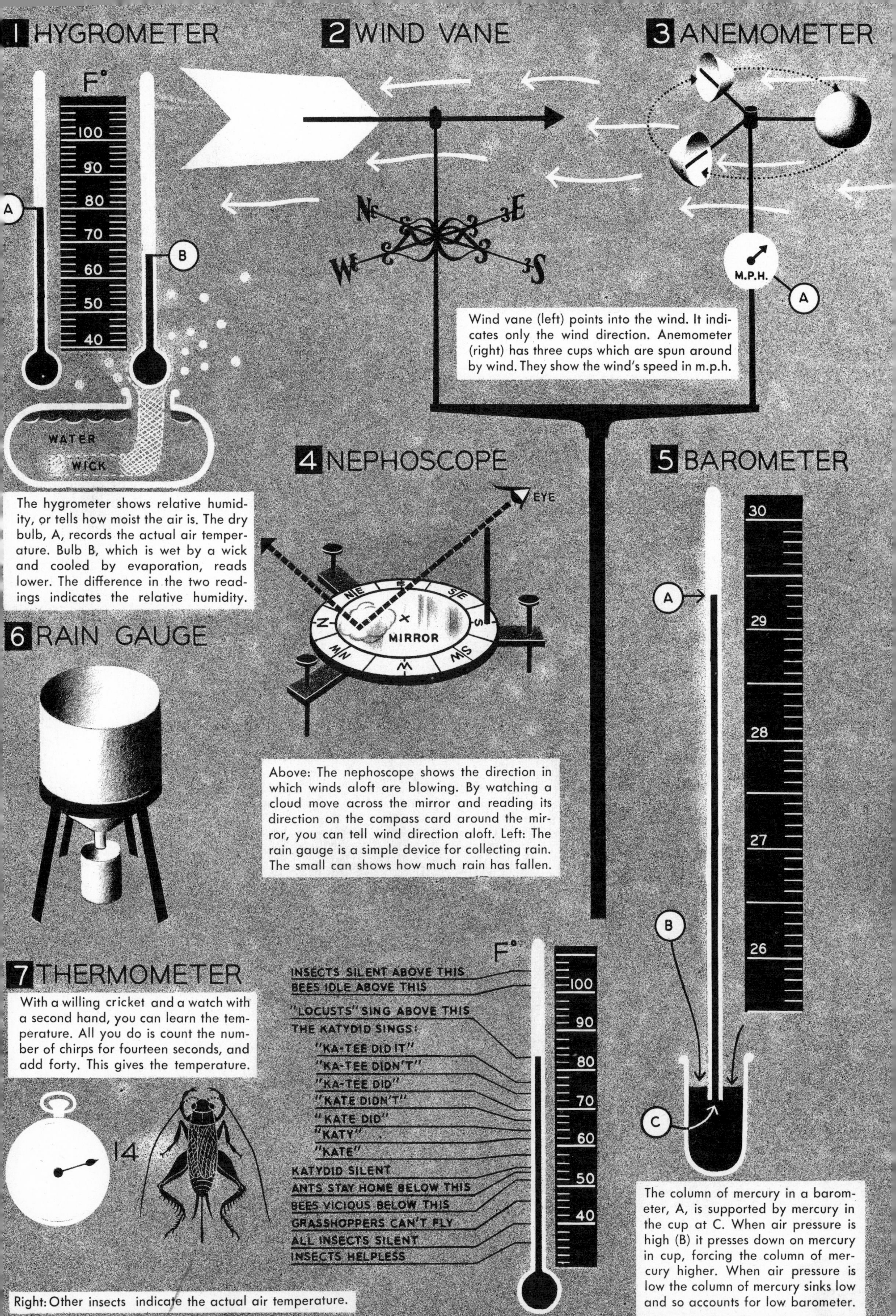

The hygrometer shows relative humidity, or tells how moist the air is. The dry bulb, A, records the actual air temperature. Bulb B, which is wet by a wick and cooled by evaporation, reads lower. The difference in the two readings indicates the relative humidity.

Wind vane (left) points into the wind. It indicates only the wind direction. Anemometer (right) has three cups which are spun around by wind. They show the wind's speed in m.p.h.

Above: The nephoscope shows the direction in which winds aloft are blowing. By watching a cloud move across the mirror and reading its direction on the compass card around the mirror, you can tell wind direction aloft. Left: The rain gauge is a simple device for collecting rain. The small can shows how much rain has fallen.

The column of mercury in a barometer, A, is supported by mercury in the cup at C. When air pressure is high (B) it presses down on mercury in cup, forcing the column of mercury higher. When air pressure is low the column of mercury sinks low and so accounts for low barometer.

With a willing cricket and a watch with a second hand, you can learn the temperature. All you do is count the number of chirps for fourteen seconds, and add forty. This gives the temperature.

Right: Other insects indicate the actual air temperature.

that sounds are carried better by moist air than by dry air, and that moist air often is a carrier of rain.

Trace in the sky the painter's brush, the winds around you soon will rush. Painter's brush refers to the high, thin cirrus clouds which usually mean that bad weather is on the way.

Rainbow at night, sailor's delight; rainbow at morning, sailor take warning. In the morning, with the sun behind you, a rainbow can mean that bad weather is moving in your direction. At dusk, when the sun is behind you, a rainbow can mean that bad weather is moving away from you. This is generally true in the mid-latitudes where weather flows from west to east.

Who originated these sayings is anyone's guess. Some of them have been with us for many years. Most likely they were created by people who depended on the sea and on farming for a livelihood. And probably they came from regions where the weather changed frequently. In areas where there is little rain and weather changes depend mostly on the seasons, you find few such sayings. Among primitive groups you find weather superstitions and weather rites like those practiced by the Pueblo Indians who live in the valley of the Rio Grande. Even today these people attempt to make it rain by performing the Green Corn Dance throughout the dry season. From morning till dusk long lines of the Indians dance over the powdery dry ground while the old men sing their rain songs to the Corn Mother, the spirit who "controls" the rain.

What an amusing picture it would be if one of our scientifically trained meteorologists were found muttering Mumbo Jumbo over his hygrometer, rain gauge, anemometer, and other weather instruments. Today's weather scientists know that a true understanding of weather will come only by slow, careful, and sometimes dangerous work. All the magic and superstition in the world can't make it rain.

At this very moment there is a team of men working a weather station on the 6280-foot peak of Mount Washington in New Hampshire. Their job is to keep a careful record of all weather changes their instruments record. In winter they are nearly always plagued with bitter weather which most of us have never experienced. The winds are so fierce that their station has to be anchored to the ground by strong steel cables. The men working the station in April 1934 once measured the

Weather station on summit of Mount Washington, New Hampshire ➝

wind at 231 miles an hour! In winter the temperature often plunges to 20°, 30°, and sometimes 40° below zero. Cold, supercooled clouds covering the peak form thick deposits of ice on the cables and building. Often the building looks like the ice-cube trays inside your refrigerator.

There are other weather scientists who risk their lives in even more dangerous ways. These are the weathermen of the air who look for hurricanes to fly into. They are battered by rain, hail, and twisting winds of 200 miles an hour. These hurricane hunters' mission is to learn more about these treacherous storms by studying what happens inside of them. Eventually their studies may teach us how to prepare ourselves for disaster like that caused by the 1938 and 1944 hurricanes which swept New England.

Before the war five German pilots decided to explore the center of a hurricane in gliders. When they flew into the storm fierce wind currents caught their planes and sucked them upward as though they were straws. The planes were broken like matchsticks. And, instead of falling, the pilots continued shooting upward into freezing heights. Only one of them came out of the vicious storm alive. His face was frozen and his fingers were smashed by bulletlike hailstones. He described his flight as an "ascent to hell."

Not all weathermen like to be as close to their work as the pioneers on Mount Washington and the hurricane hunters. For every adventurous weather explorer there are hundreds whose routine job it is to record the daily temperature, humidity, wind speeds, cloud movements, and rainfall. As unexciting as their work might seem, these men are vital to the Weather Bureau. By teletype machine they send their readings to weather stations all over the country. By recording these readings on his daily weather map your local weatherman tells you what kind of weather to expect tomorrow.

To understand how the weatherman arrives at his forecast of "Hail, thunderstorms, and lightning," we will first explore the thin blanket of air that shields our planet against the torturous cold of outer space. For it is within our atmosphere that all weather is born: hurricanes, tornadoes, and gentle sea breezes. With an understanding of what the atmosphere is made of and how it behaves, you will be closer to answering the question, "What is weather?"

our ocean of air

In a way, man is like the creatures who live at the bottom of the sea. Draw them up to the surface and they will die. Accustomed to the inky black depths and the hundreds of tons of water pressing against them, they are comfortably at home. Like these ocean creatures, man also lives in a sea. Only man's sea is a sea of air 75 times deeper than the deepest ocean and nearly 100 times higher than the loftiest mountain.

Held captive by earth's gravity, the atmosphere surrounds our planet to a depth of 300 to 700 miles. Take our atmosphere away, and there would be no trees, no animals, no life of any kind. There would be no weather, no clouds or colorful sunsets, and no sound. For it is the atmosphere which carries sound waves to our ears where "noise" is created. No atmosphere would mean a deathlike stillness and an eternally black sky. By day the direct rays of the sun would heat everything on earth to the boiling point of water. And by night we would freeze in temperatures plunging to 300 degrees below zero.

As a greenhouse protects the plants it houses, our atmosphere protects us from the sun's burning heat and the night's freezing cold. Long after the sun has set, the atmosphere serves as a blanket and prevents the earth's stored-up heat from escaping into outer space.

Many of us are not in the habit of thinking of the air as matter, as something that can be weighed. But as surely as iron and stone can be weighed, so can our air. If it were possible to press the earth's air into

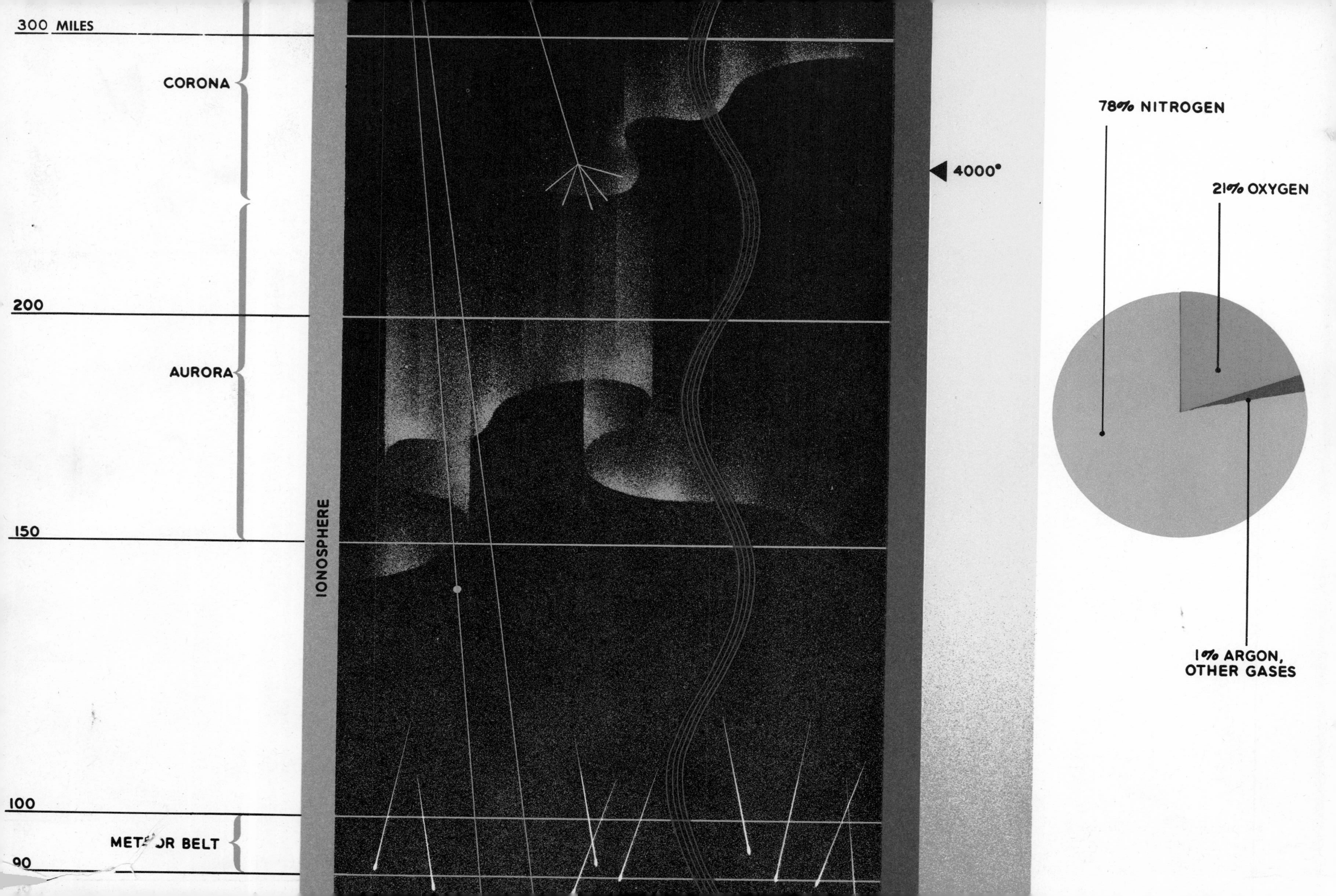
300 MILES
CORONA
200
AURORA
150
IONOSPHERE
100
MET OR BELT
90
4000°
78% NITROGEN
21% OXYGEN
1% ARGON,
OTHER GASES

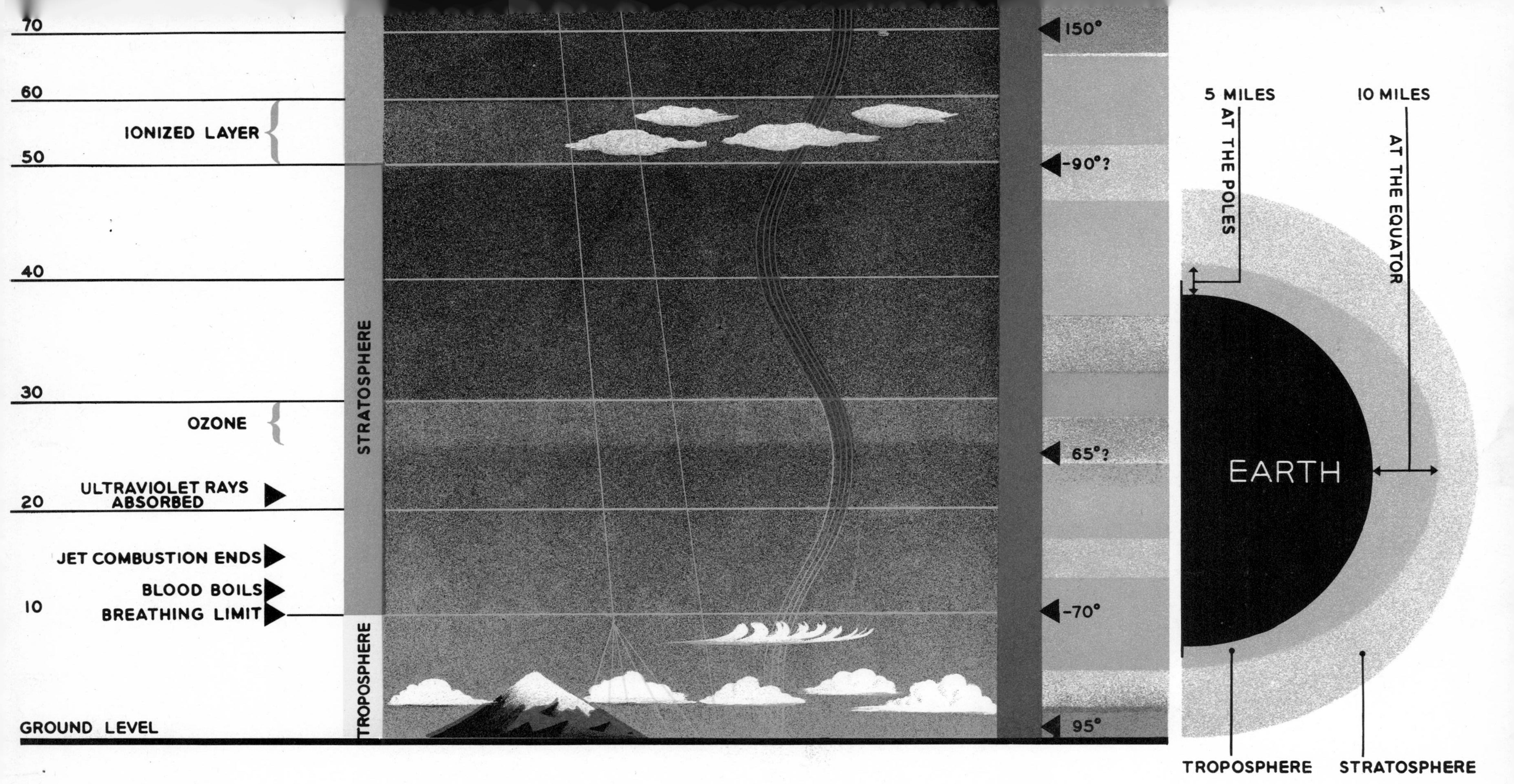

Man lives at the bottom of a deep ocean of air. At ground level the air is a dense mixture of gases. The higher you go the "thinner" the air becomes. At what altitude the last thin traces of atmosphere are found, no one knows for sure. It may be as high as five thousand or six thousand miles. The lowest layer of air is called the troposphere. All the world's weather occurs in this layer. The next major layer is the stratosphere. At the top of this layer the air is so thin that the sky is nearly black. Above the stratosphere is the ionosphere, the top of which is the border line of space. The air around us protects us from the bitter coldness of outer space. It also shields us from a continuous bombardment of meteorites. As meteors strike our atmosphere, they are burned up by friction heat. The air also filters out most of the cosmic rays and ultraviolet rays from the sun. If these rays reached us in full force, our lives would be endangered. (See page 13 for a description of the air ocean.)

a huge block and put it on a set of scales it would weigh about 5,900,000,000,000,000 tons (five quadrillion, nine hundred trillion).

The air we live in is a mixture of gases and dust. Seventy-eight per cent of it is made up of nitrogen, the gas which is so important as a food for plants. Most of the remaining gas, 21 per cent, is oxygen, which animals and men alike depend on for life. The remaining 1 per cent is a blend of other gases—argon, helium, neon, ozone, carbon dioxide, and still others. In addition to these gases the air is swarming with tiny dust particles: salt crystals from oceans, dust from rocks and sand, pollen from plants, ash from volcanoes, and dust which drifts in from outer space.

All of these gases and dust particles press down on us and against us from all sides with a tremendous weight. Right now more than a ton of air is pressing against you. Yet, like fish living near the floor of the sea, you are unaware of this great weight because your body is made to withstand it. This heavy pressure comes from the motion of molecules of which all things are made. These particles are so small that not even the strongest microscope show them to us.

Near the surface of the ground the air pressure is the strongest. The higher you go, the weaker the pressure becomes. Our atmosphere blankets the earth in layers, each one pressing down on the layers below and packing the air molecules closely together. Like bugs darting and bumping around an electric-light bulb, the molecules dart back and forth and bump against our bodies. It is this constant bombardment that makes us feel pressure and heat. The higher we go into the atmosphere, the looser the molecules are packed. For this reason the pressure at high altitudes is less than it is at sea level. We say that the air becomes "thinner." Because the many layers of air are constantly pressing down on other layers below, one half of the earth's atmosphere is squeezed into the first three and a half miles above us. At what altitude the last thin traces of atmosphere are found, no one knows for sure. It may be as high as 5000 or 6000 miles.

Man can live only in the lower levels of the earth's atmosphere. If he tried to explore the upper regions of the air without the protection of pressure suits and oxygen masks he would gasp for breath as a fish gasps when it is taken from its watery home. By exploring high altitudes man has learned that life is possible only within the first three and a half

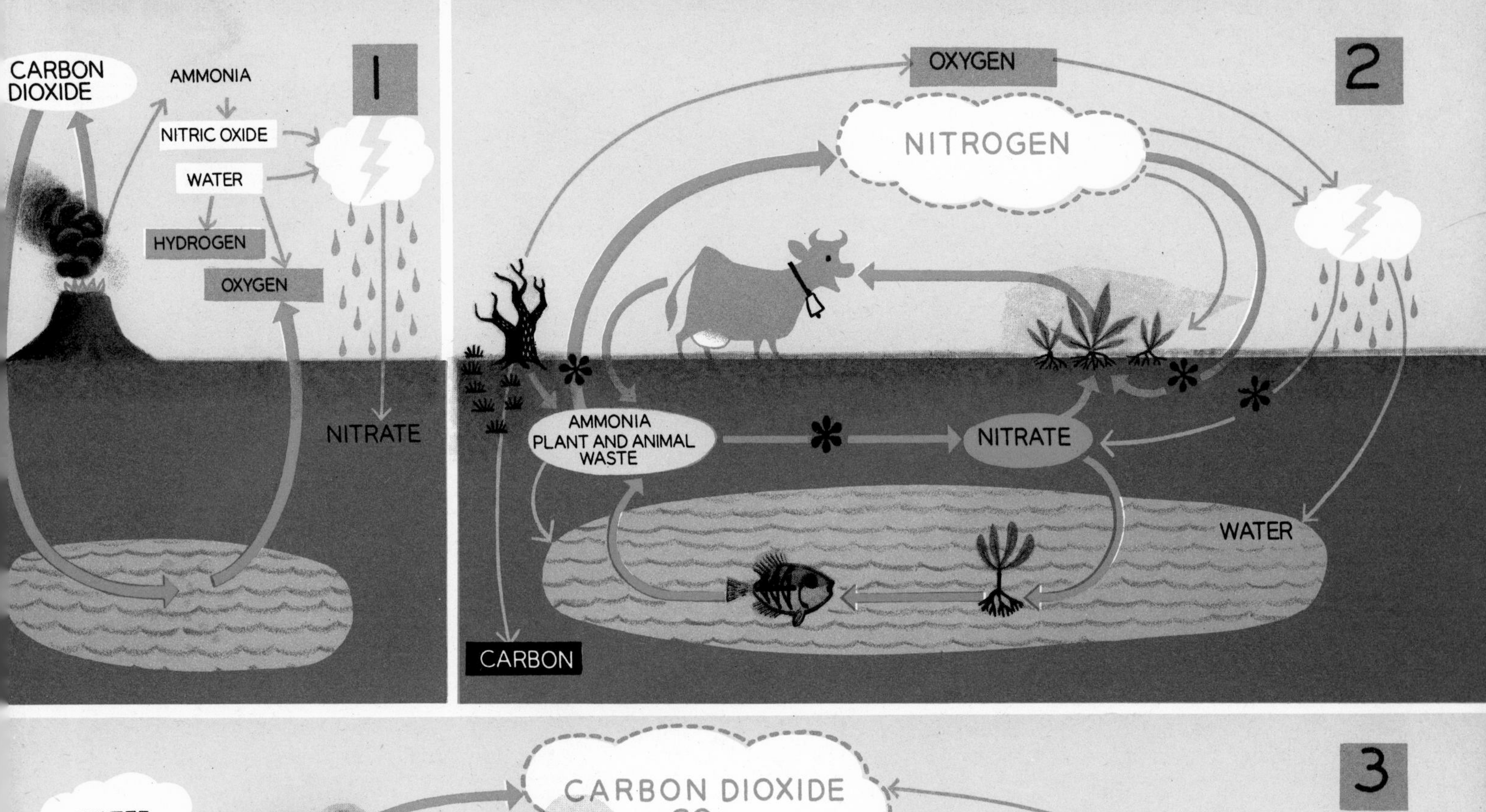

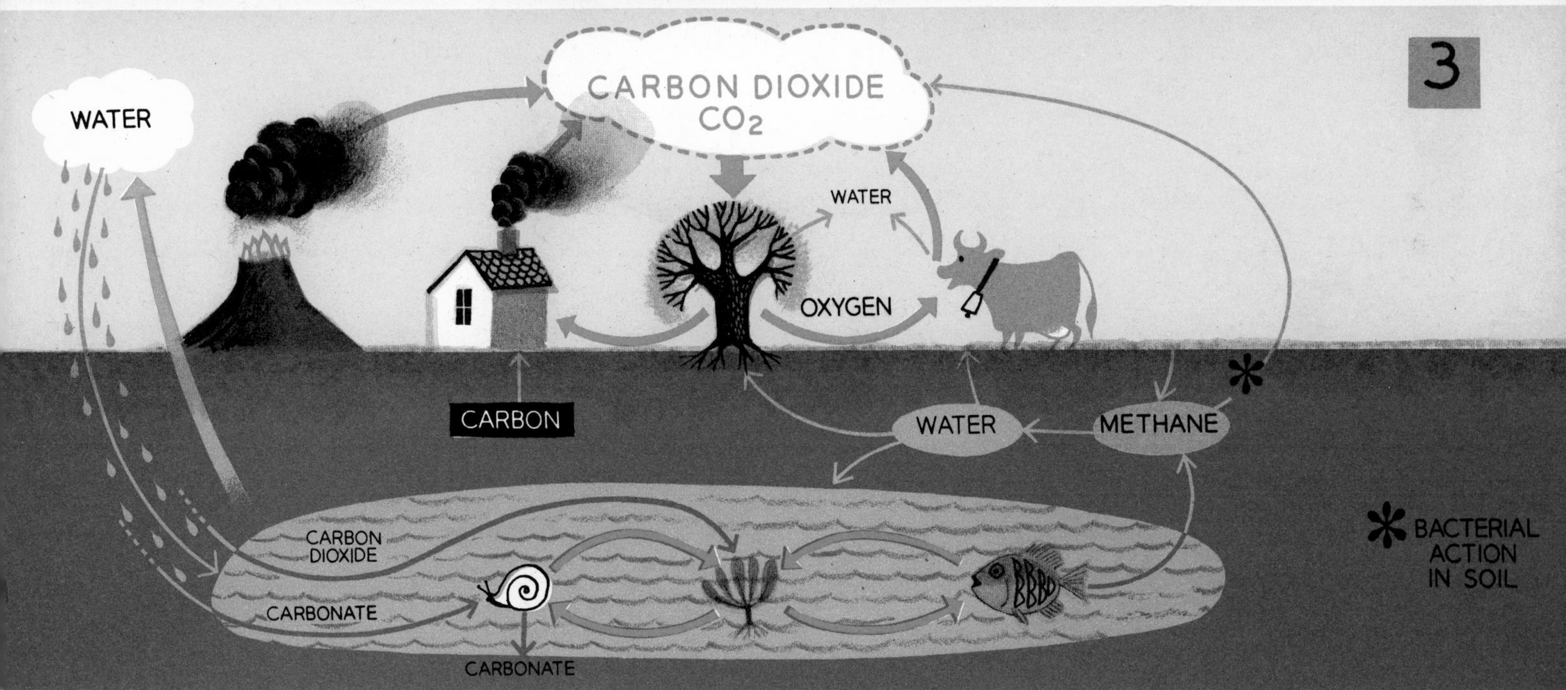

miles above our planet. Nearly all of the earth's people live within the first mile above sea level.

For many years men thought that the air became colder with higher altitudes. But the new science of meteorology is teaching us that our early beliefs were wrong. Balloons and rockets carrying sensitive weather instruments high into the atmosphere show us that the air surrounding our planet is composed of layers, or shells. And each layer has its own pressure and temperature oddities which make it different from the others.

the troposphere

The first and lowest of these layers is called the "troposphere." It is the most crowded with gas molecules and is where all of our weather is found. Over the United States the troposphere reaches up to 40,000 feet, nearly eight miles. Air Force pilots have found that the higher they fly into the troposphere, the colder the air becomes. On a hot summer day the bottom of this air layer may be 95°. But at the top of the troposphere the temperature dips to a frigid low of nearly 70° below zero. This air layer cools off at an average rate of 3.5° for every 1000 feet of altitude.

The reason for its cooling can be found in your kitchen when the oven is on. The air closest to the stove is the hottest. But as you move away, the air becomes cooler. Acting like a stove, the sun-heated earth warms only the air near its surface.

We also know the troposphere for its winds and air currents. At the top of this air layer the wind blows constantly at 150 to 200 miles an hour. In addition to winds the troposphere is filled with air currents which move up and down. Glider pilots search for these currents and ride them aloft as though they were in an elevator. As the sun heats large flat patches of land, the air above becomes lighter, rises, and creates these "thermal currents."

the tropopause

Resting on top of the troposphere is the "tropopause," our planet's second layer of air. Here the temperature does not drop any lower than the frigid air just beneath. At this level, however, the winds reach their greatest force. World War II pilots flying at near-tropopause altitudes over Japan came back with stories of "jet-stream" winds up to 300 miles an hour.

the stratosphere

The third layer of air is called the "stratosphere." It begins where the tropopause ends and reaches to a height of about 55 miles. The lower regions of the stratosphere, like the tropopause, are swept with strong winds and are icy cold. But at higher altitudes the winds begin to weaken and finally die. At about 25 miles aloft, higher than any of our rocket planes have flown, something strange begins to happen. The air begins to turn warm. Possibly it climbs to a comfortable 60° or 70° above zero, but our meteorologists are not certain. The cause of this sudden warming is a layer of gas called "ozone," without which man would find it difficult to live on earth. The ozone layer stops the sun's ultraviolet rays from reaching us in full force. While a few of these rays are good for us, too many of them would soon kill us.

Beyond the ozone layer, at a height of about 50 miles, the temperature again becomes cold. Near the top of the stratosphere it plunges to at least 30° below zero, and possibly as low as −100°. Also, near the top of the stratosphere the sky is nearly black. At these heights the thinning air does not reflect as much of the sun's light as the lower dense atmosphere does. Even during the day, at this altitude the stars shine steadily as they do from the moon, which has no atmosphere.

the ionosphere

Above the stratosphere is the "ionosphere," the top of which is the border line of space. At its lower level, around 50 to 60 miles above the earth, we find the misty "golden fire" of the noctilucent clouds. These clouds may be thin whisps of ice crystals or dust coming from meteors or volcanic ash. They are called "noctilucent" because they can be seen shining high in the heavens long after the sun has set. In 1883, when the volcanic island of Krakatoa shook the earth in a mighty explosion, people around the world saw these golden mist clouds. Dust from the explosion drifted through the atmosphere to heights of 50 to 60 miles and hung there for several months.

At the lower levels of the ionosphere the temperature begins to rise again. At 70 miles up it may be between 100° and 200° above zero. And at 250 miles aloft it may reach as high as 4000°! But you should not confuse this kind of "heat" with the heat you feel when your backyard thermometer reads 97°. High-altitude heat is simply a way of expressing the speed of gas molecules. Since there are fewer gas molecules at high altitudes, they are free to bounce around faster than the crowded molecules around us at sea level. Actually, at an altitude of 250 miles any living creature exposed to the air would die by being broiled to death and frozen to death at the same time. That part of him facing the sun would be broiled while the part in shadow would be frozen.

Topping the ionosphere is the last layer of air between us and outer space. Called the "fountain layer," it may reach up into the black sky as high as 5000 miles. As a water sprinkler shoots a fine spray into the air, in the fountain layer the ever-thinning gas particles behave much the same way. So for the weather man the fountain layer is the "top of the world." Beyond is the cold, black emptiness of outer space.

how the air circulates

Like the sea, our ocean of air is constantly in motion. Many forces acting on it bring us the "prevailing winds," which blow steadily day and night, and hurricanes which strike suddenly, then die a few hours later.

The sun is one of the forces that keeps the atmosphere in motion. Its rays shine the hottest on that wide belt of sea and land we call the equa-

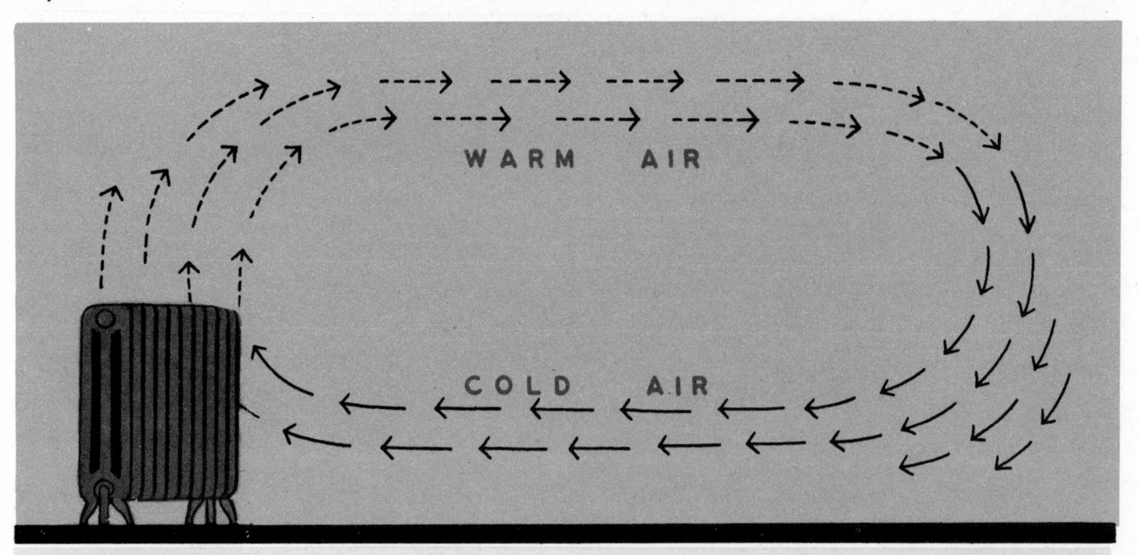

Heat from a radiator warms the air near it, pushes it toward the ceiling. Cooler air near the floor flows toward the radiator to replace rising air. In this way the air is kept moving.

tor. As air above the equator becomes heated it rises, as air above a hot radiator is pushed up toward the ceiling. When the equator's hot air rises high enough to be cooled by freezing temperatures aloft, it grows heavy and tries to settle back to the ground. But the endless stream of hot air pushing up from below prevents it from settling. So in great arcs

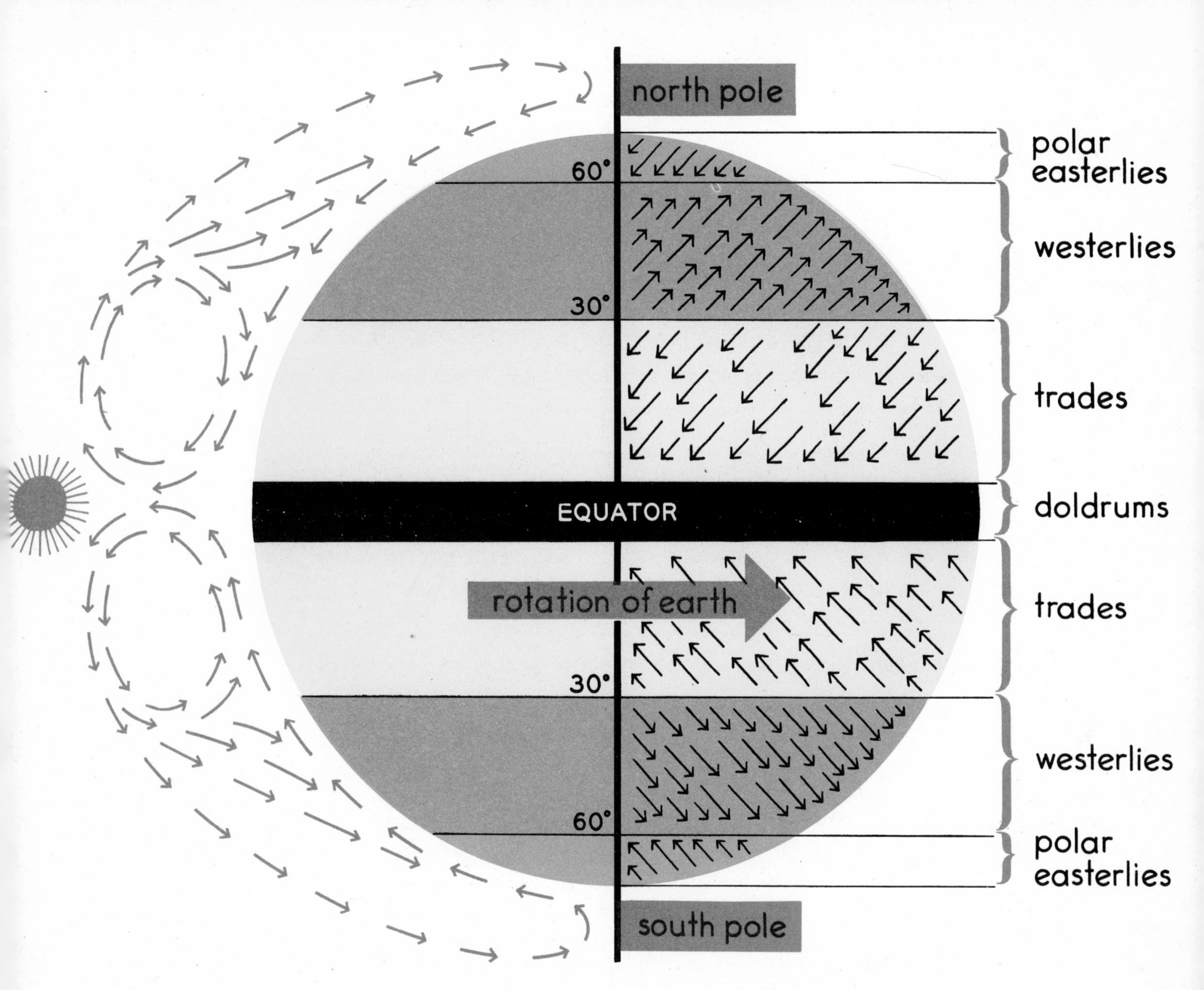

The air enclosing our planet is set in motion by heat from the sun. As air above the equator becomes heated, it rises and flows off toward poles. Spinning earth causes wind belts.

it moves off toward the North and South Poles. When it reaches latitudes of about 30° some of the air settles to the ground, where it is caught by winds rushing toward the equator. The rest continues on toward the polar regions where it, too, finally curves groundward and makes a return trip to the equator.

So the earth's atmosphere can be thought of as two large conveyer belts. Each belt stretches up from the equator. Then one loops up toward the North Pole and curves back to the equator while the other loops down toward the South Pole and completes its circle. Meteorologists would be happy if the air-circulation picture were that simple. But a second force complicates things—the spinning of the earth.

Spinning at about 16 miles a minute, the earth's surface deflects the loops of air passing over it. So, instead of having constant winds that blow straight from the equator to the poles and back again, we have winds that blow on a slant.

At the equator the air above the earth moves along at the speed of the earth's surface. For this reason there is not much wind. Sailors of old dreaded this area which they called the "doldrums." For days on end they would sit motionless with no breeze to fill their sails. As the hot air rises from the equator it picks up moisture from the sea. As the air is carried into cold altitudes it cools and releases its moisture in the form of rain. So hot moist air and heavy rain, like that found in southern Asia and the "fever swamps" of Africa, are typical of the equator's climate.

As air from the equator streams toward the Poles some of it breaks away and flows down to the surface at about 30° latitude. Here it piles up and forms a high-pressure belt, which at sea is called the "horse

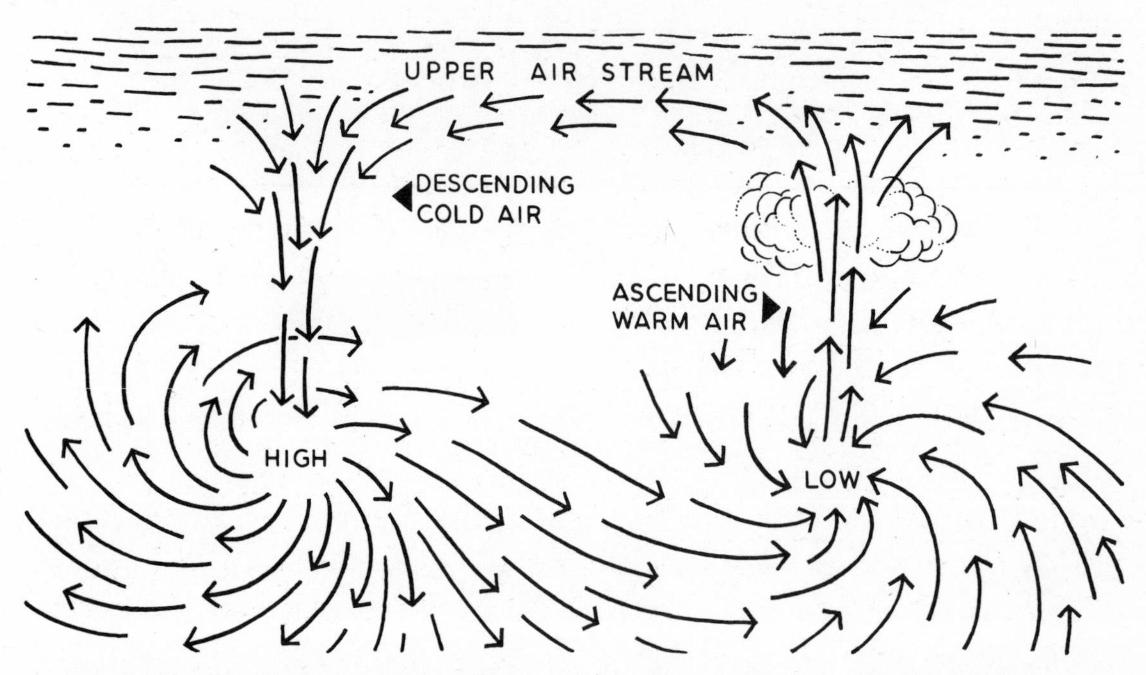

Left: Cool air flowing down from the upper air stream piles up and forms a high-pressure system.
Right: Warm air which rises into the air stream above leaves a low-pressure system over land, sea.

latitudes." At this point the air doubles back and rushes toward the equator to replace air rising aloft. The winds resulting from this equator-bound air flow are called the "trade winds" and blow steadily both day and night. In the Northern Hemisphere they blow from northeast to southwest. And in the Southern Hemisphere their direction is southeast to northwest.

Weather in the horse latitudes is generally hot, dry, and sunny with little rain. The land area along this belt has the world's great deserts, the North American prairies and the steppes of Russia. No one is quite sure where the name "horse latitudes" comes from. One writer says that the name comes from the old sailing days. Ships carrying horses were often becalmed at these latitudes, and the crew had to push the animals overboard when the fresh-water supply ran too low.

Beyond the horse latitudes to about 60° north and south is another belt of winds called the "prevailing westerlies." In the Northern Hemisphere they blow from southwest to northeast, and in the Southern Hemisphere from northwest to southeast. (In the weatherman's language, by the way, a westerly wind is one that blows *from* the west, not into the west.) The prevailing westerlies are caused by a great flow of Poleward-bound air traveling faster than the spinning surface of the earth. At altitudes where our air liners fly, the westerlies blow steadily. So a plane flying from San Francisco to New York can usually make better time than one flying from New York to San Francisco.

At lower altitudes the westerlies are less dependable. Cold, dry air moving down from the north and warm, moist air moving up from the south meet in the path of the westerlies. The results are ever-changing wind currents, tornadoes, hurricanes, hail, sleet and snow, all of which make the region of the westerlies the most active weather belt on earth.

From latitude 60° to the Poles the flow of air is again slowed down. The result is a third belt of winds called the "polar easterlies." So when the flow of hot moist air which began at the equator reaches its polar destinations it is cool and dry as it settles to the surface. From here it spreads out and begins its return journey to the equator, where the cycle will begin again.

What has all this talk about the atmosphere, doldrums, trade winds, prevailing westerlies, and polar easterlies to do with the weather? Everything. Before we can understand how a hurricane or tornado is put together, how a cloud is formed, or why the weatherman may predict snow for the Fourth of July, we must first examine our ocean of air and the restless currents moving within it. Now that we have had that look we can try to solve a few meteorological mysteries and learn why the daily weather sometimes behaves in such strange and unpleasant ways.

weather in the making

Before you begin reading this chapter, go into the kitchen and pour yourself a glass of ice water, but don't drink it. Bring it back and put it down beside you. You'll be performing an experiment that will help you understand something important about the weather.

By some quirk of nature we are fortunate enough to be living on a slightly tipsy planet. In relation to the sun our planet does not hang perfectly straight in space. Instead it is tilted, with the North and South Poles shooting off at an angle instead of pointing straight up and down, or as the astronomer says, the earth has an inclination of 23.5°. Because the earth is tilted, we have seasons. In winter the sun's rays strike the Northern Hemisphere at an angle, because this part of our globe is tipped away from the sun. Hence cool weather with snow in the north. But in summer because the sun's rays point nearly straight down on the Northern Hemisphere, we have hot weather. By keeping a record of how the sun travels across the sky, you can see how it strikes us from different angles as the seasons change. In winter it traces an arc low across the sky from east to west. In summer its arc swings high overhead. For this reason summer days are longer. And because they are longer, the earth has more time to store up the sun's heat and reflect it back into the atmosphere to bring us hot days and sleepless nights.

At this point you may be interested to know that the hottest day on earth was September 13, 1922, in Azizia, Libya. The mercury rose to

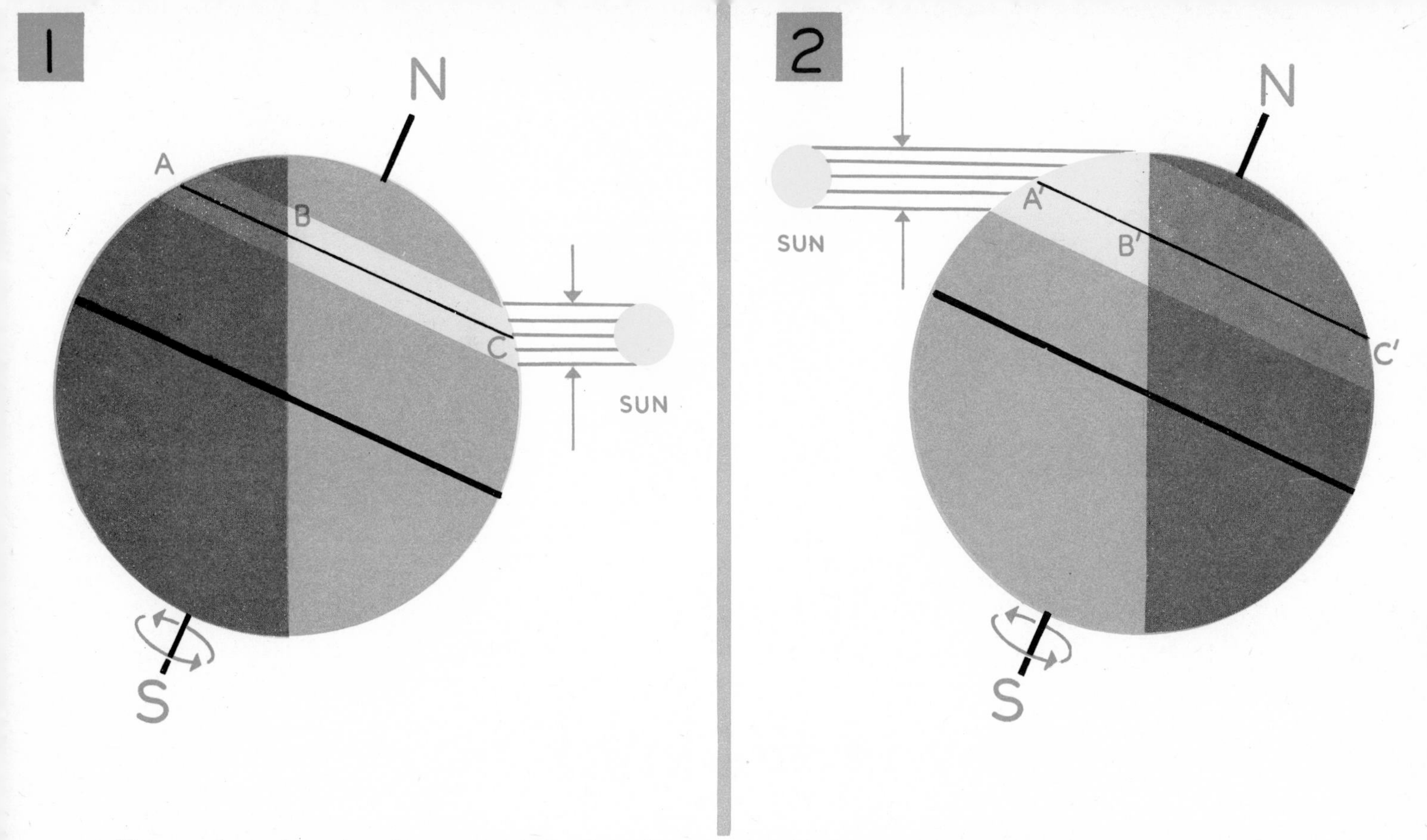

Diagram above shows how in summer and in winter the sun strikes the earth at different angles. In summer the sun shines nearly straight down on us, gives us hot weather. In winter the sun's rays strike us at an angle so we have cool weather.

Diagram shows how the sun swings lower, then higher overhead during a year. From high summer position it swings lower (autumn), then to lowest (winter). Next it climbs (spring) and finally returns to its high position in the sky to bring summer.

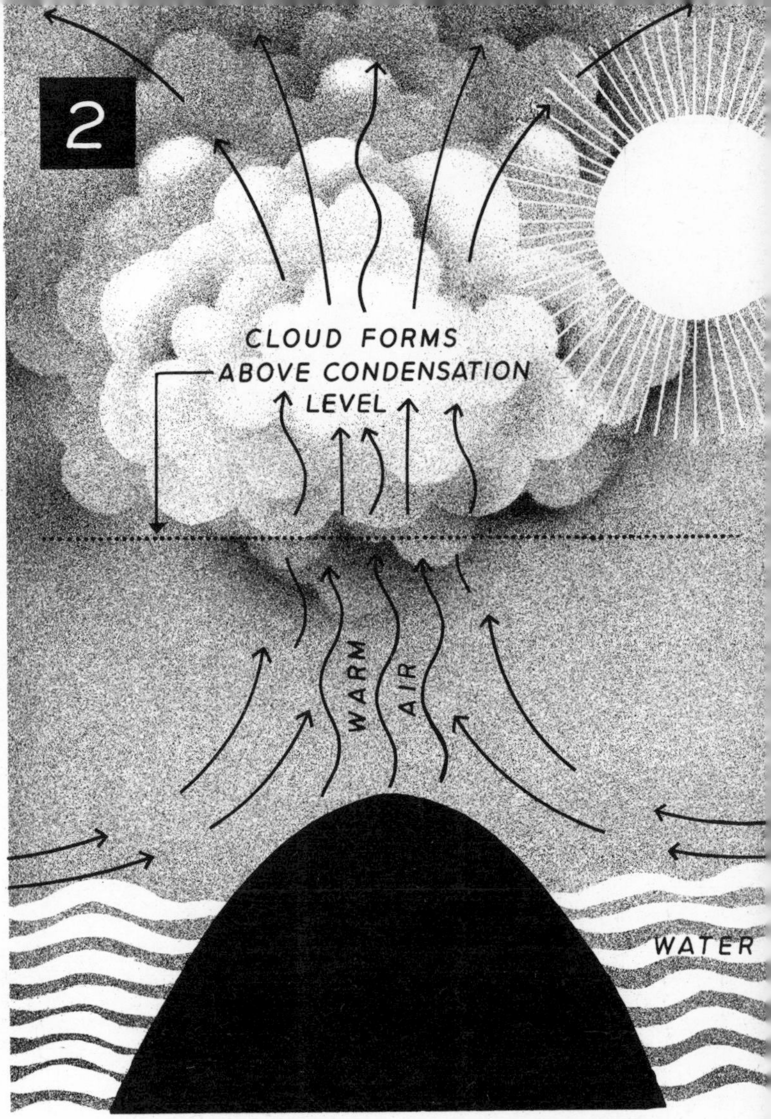

1. On a calm night, cool air aloft, which is heavier than the warmer air below, flows down mountain, mixes with warm air, creating fog.

2. Vertical winds, or thermal currents, are formed when land air heated by the sun rises. Air from the surrounding area rushes in.

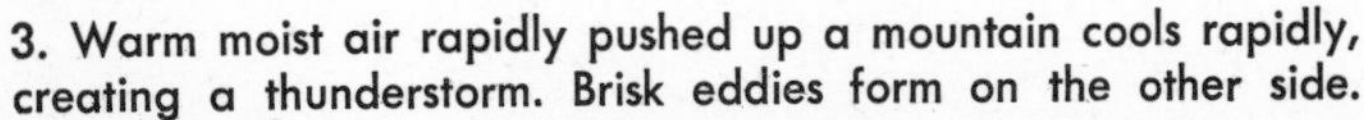

3. Warm moist air rapidly pushed up a mountain cools rapidly, creating a thunderstorm. Brisk eddies form on the other side.

4. A tornado is formed when very cold air comes in contact with very warm air. The warm air spirals aloft swiftly, creating a tornado.

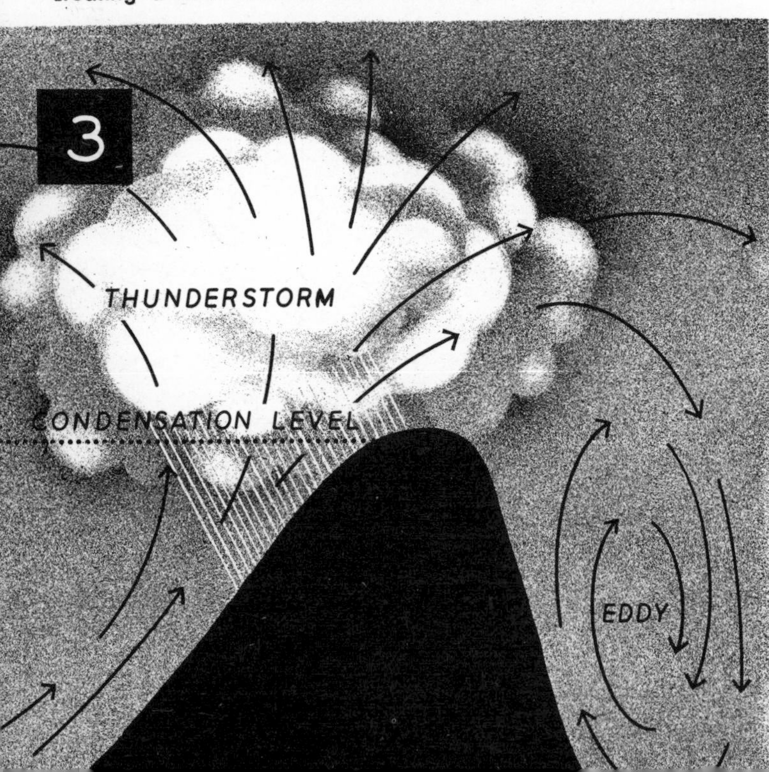

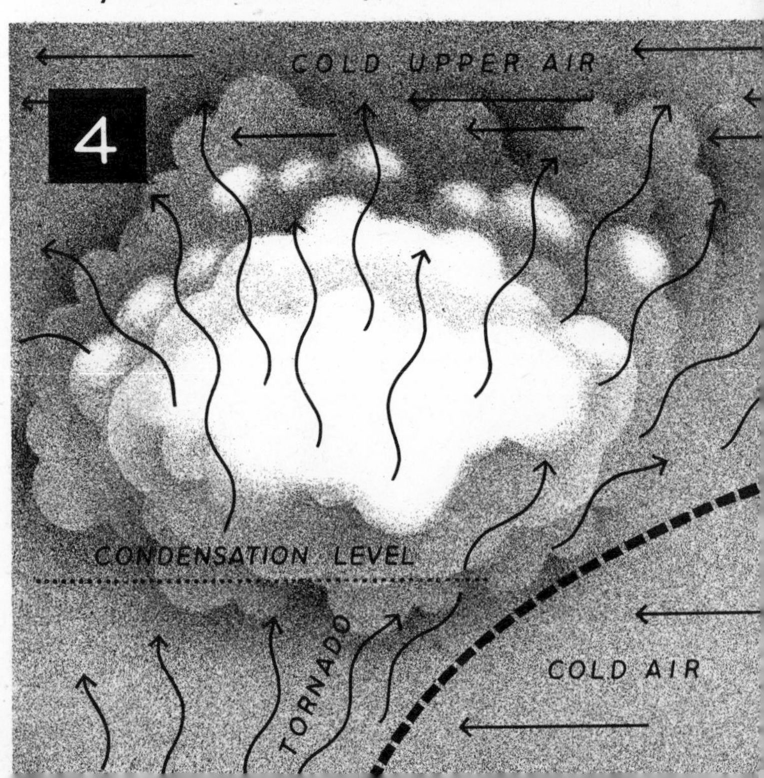

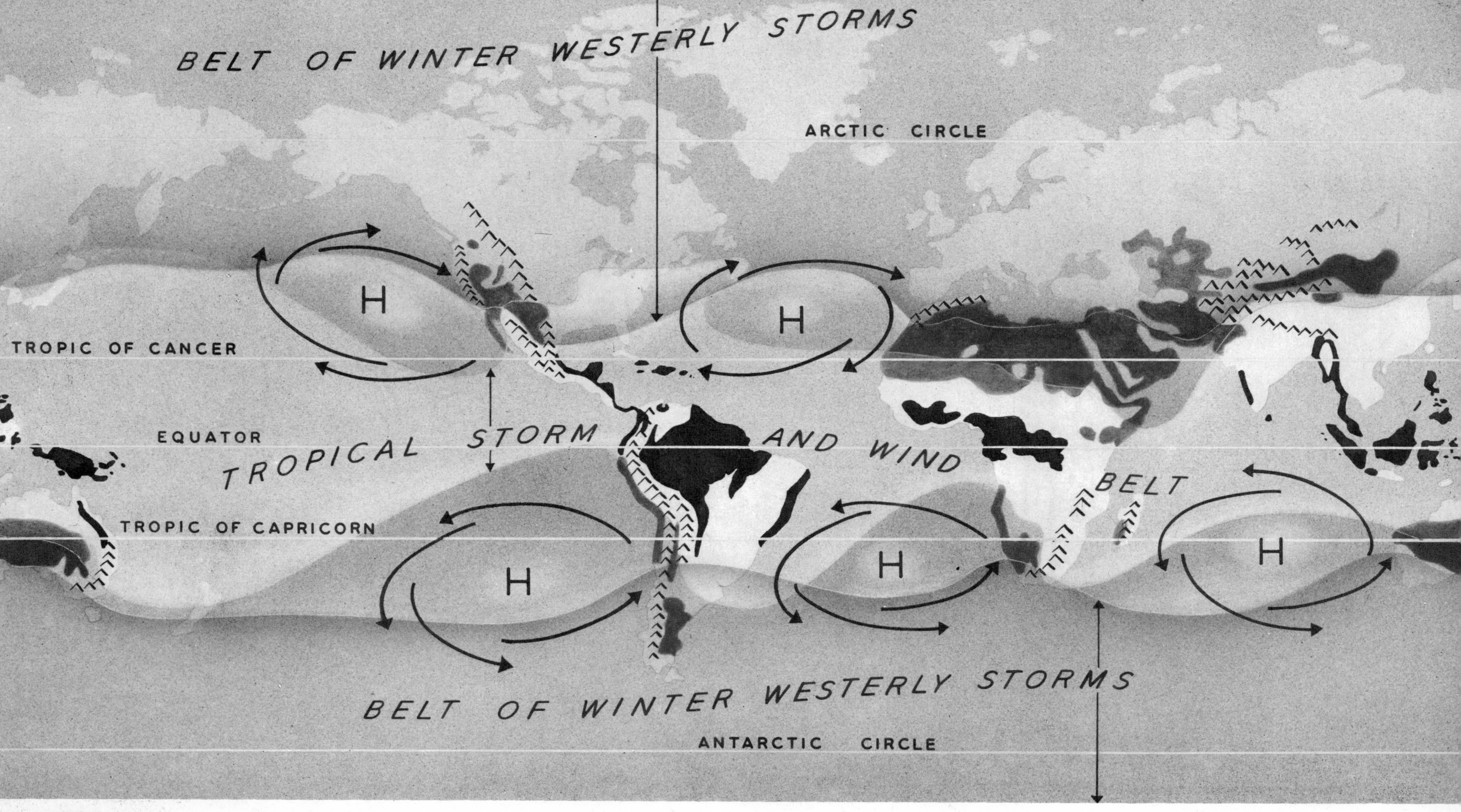

This map shows how desert areas and wet areas are distributed around the globe north and south of the equator. At about 30 degrees north and south latitudes the air aloft sweeps down and piles up to create areas of high pressure. Weather along these belts is mostly hot, dry, and sunny. The world's great deserts (dark patches on map) are found along the horse latitudes. Sandwiched between the horse latitudes is the equator. Along this belt the world's rain forests, or "fever swamps," (black patches on map) are plagued with hot moist air, heavy rain.

136°, even in the shade! The highest the temperature has ever been recorded in the United States is 134°. This was the official reading at Greenland Ranch, Death Valley, July 10, 1913. At the other extreme the Russians in 1938 reported a frigid low of 108° below zero in Siberia. The record low in the United States is 66° below, reported by the Riverside Ranger Station in Yellowstone Park on February 9, 1933.

How hot you are in the summer and how cold you are in the winter depend largely on whether you live inland or near the sea. On many hot summer days probably you've seen a dog dig a shallow trench and then lie in it to cool off. To a depth of a few inches, the earth hungrily

soaks up the sun's heat, but just below the surface the ground stays cool, even on the hottest days. Unlike the ground, the sea absorbs the sun's heat evenly and deeply. This is why water stays warm (or cool) longer than the ground does. Soon after sunset the ground quickly gives up its heat, but the temperature of the water changes little. All during the summer oceans and lakes slowly become warmer and warmer while the land heats by day and cools at night. By the time winter approaches the sea is warmer than the land, so it begins to give up some of its stored heat. Air warmed by the sea flows inland and so accounts for "mild" winters along the New England coast in comparison with the cold winters in Vermont and Montana.

A sea breeze is created when hot air over the land rises. Cool sea air flows in to take its place.

A land breeze is created when warm air over the sea rises. Cool land air flows out over the sea.

wind

The "sea breeze" which people along the coast look forward to on summer afternoons is caused by hot air rising from the land. As the air above the land is warmed it expands, becomes lighter, and rises. Cooler air from the ocean then rushes in to replace the air which is rising. Result, a sea breeze. At night just the opposite happens and a "land breeze" is created. Cool air over the water is heated, expands, and rises. Air from the land then rushes toward the sea. The meteorologist calls these warm parcels of air "low-pressure areas" because the gas molecules are spaced far apart. Cool air parcels whose molecules are packed closely together are "high-pressure areas."

Chicago, even though it is not near the sea, often benefits from "sea breezes." Nearby Lake Michigan is responsible. On one hot afternoon in 1901 people in Chicago watched the thermometer climb to 102°. As the land warmed, hot air rising over the city drew in cooler air from the lake. Within an hour the temperature dropped 18°.

Wind, then, is simply air in motion, air which is rushing from an area of high pressure toward an area of low pressure. When the weatherman reports the winds to us he uses a measuring system worked out in 1805 by Admiral Beaufort. For example, a "moderate breeze" is a wind of 13 to 18 miles an hour. A "fresh gale" is a wind of 39 to 46 miles an hour. And a "hurricane" is any wind more than 75 miles an hour. Admiral Beaufort even went so far as to tell us how to measure the wind's speed in miles an hour without using special instruments. A moderate breeze, he said, is one which moves dust, loose paper, and small branches. And a fresh gale is wind which breaks twigs off trees and makes walking difficult. While the Beaufort wind scale is a fine standard for the amateur meteorologist, the weatherman prefers his "anemometer," a special instrument made of four small cups which catch the wind and are spun around in a circle. The anemometer accurately measures the wind speed in miles per hour.

water vapor

Riding on the winds and hanging in motionless air is a form of water which the meteorologist calls "water vapor." On hot, muggy days and whenever you take a shower the air around you is laden with water vapor. All day long as the sun shines on lakes, oceans, and puddles, it changes some of the water into vapor and so the air is moistened. The hotter the air is, the more water vapor it can hold. Cold air can hold little water vapor. The next time you take a hot bath or shower, notice how moist the air in the bathroom becomes. As water sprays out of the shower, some of it turns into water vapor. Gradually so much of it passes into the air that the air can't hold any more. At this point you notice that the

BEAUFORT NUMBERS:	MAP SYMBOL FOR WIND SPEED AND DIRECTION: (←---------)	SPEED: M.P.H.	DESCRIPTION:	SPECIFICATIONS:
0			CALM	SMOKE RISES VERTICALLY.
1	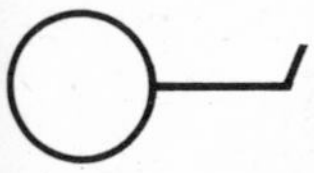	1 TO 3	LIGHT AIR	WIND DIRECTION SHOWN BY DRIFT OF SMOKE.
2	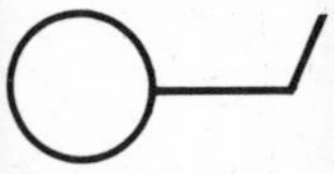	4 TO 7	SLIGHT BREEZE	WIND FELT ON FACE; LEAVES RUSTLE; FLAG STIRS.
3	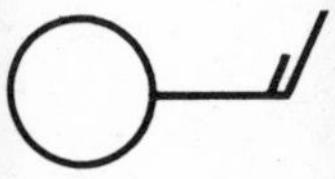	8 TO 12	GENTLE BREEZE	LEAVES AND TWIGS IN CONSTANT MOTION; WIND EXTENDS LIGHT FLAGS.
4	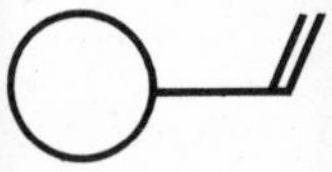	13 TO 18	MODERATE BREEZE	DUST, LOOSE PAPER, AND SMALL BRANCHES ARE MOVED; FLAGS FLAP.
5	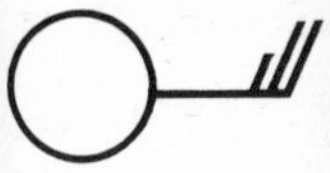	19 TO 24	FRESH BREEZE	SMALL TREES IN LEAF BEGIN TO SWAY; FLAGS RIPPLE.
6	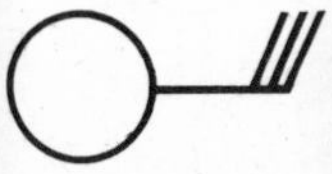	25 TO 31	STRONG BREEZE	LARGE BRANCHES IN MOTION; WHISTLING TELEGRAPH WIRES; FLAGS BEAT.
7	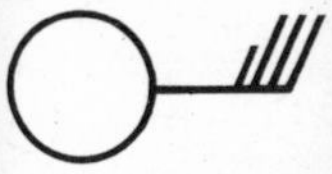	32 TO 38	MODERATE GALE	WHOLE TREES IN MOTION; FLAGS ARE EXTENDED.
8		39 TO 46	FRESH GALE	TWIGS BREAK OFF TREES; WALKING IS HINDERED.
9	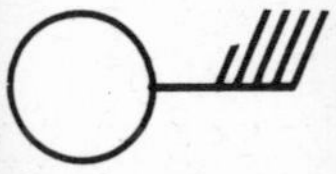	47 TO 54	STRONG GALE	SLIGHT DAMAGE TO HOUSES.
10	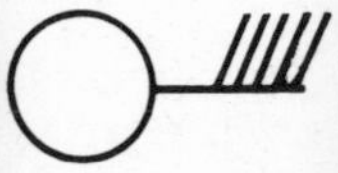	55 TO 63	WHOLE GALE	TREES UPROOTED; MUCH DAMAGE TO HOUSES.
11	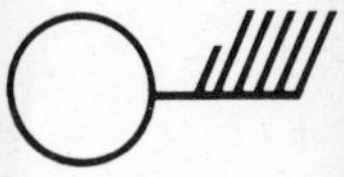	64 TO 75	STORM	WIDESPREAD DAMAGE.
12	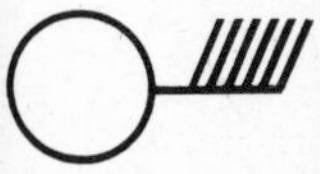	OVER 75	HURRICANE	EXCESSIVE DAMAGE.

mirror and window become all cloudy. What happens is that the overflow of water vapor condenses, or turns back into water, as it strikes the mirror, window, and walls.

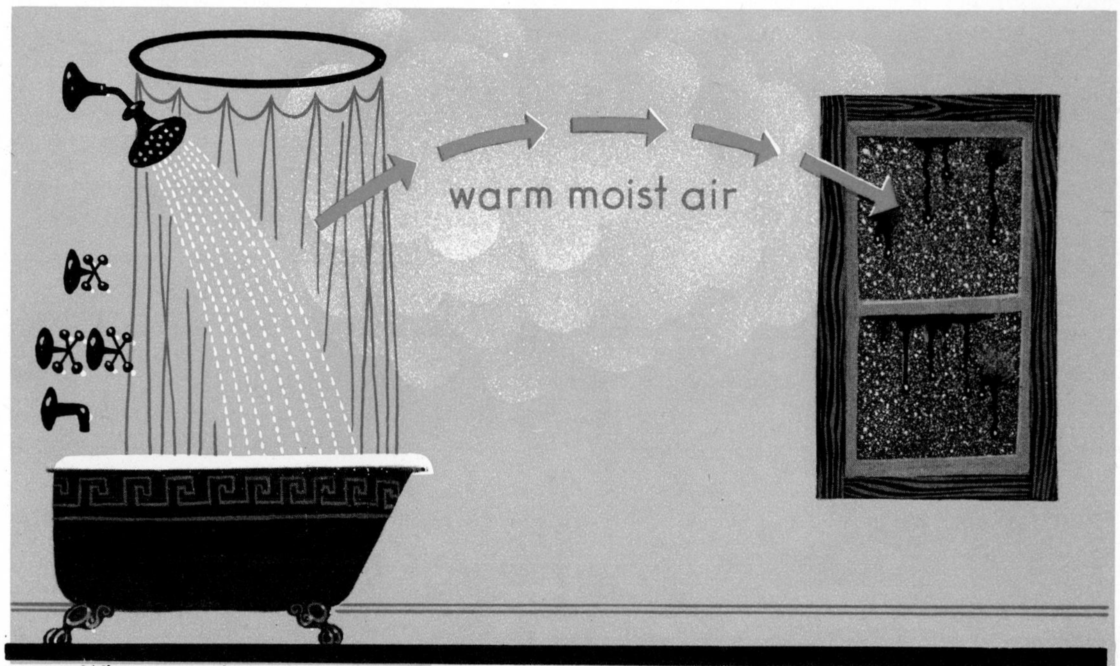

When you take a shower you fill the room with warm moist air containing water vapor. As air cools, it gives up moisture, so you find it condensing to water on window and mirror.

At night cool ground and plants chill warm air. As air cools, it is forced to give up some of its water vapor. Striking the cool plants, the water vapor condenses into dew droplets.

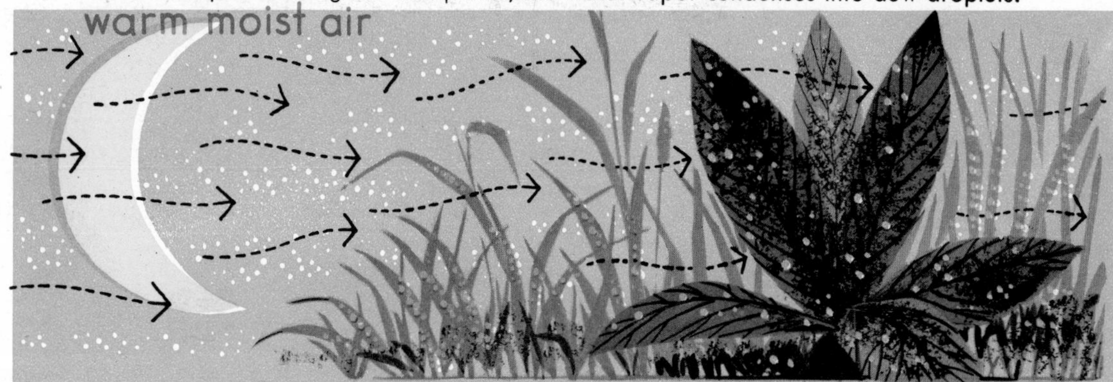

On summer nights when the ground becomes chilled, grass and plants cool the air flowing around them. As the air is cooled it is forced to give up some of its water vapor. The result is evening and morning dew. In the fall, when the night temperature drops to freezing, you find morning frost instead of dew. The low temperature changes the tiny water droplets into ice crystals.

About now it should be time to examine that glass of ice water you poured at the beginning of this chapter. If the water was cold enough, the glass should now be covered with your own homemade dew. How did water from the inside of the glass get to the outside? It didn't. The cold glass cooled the air around it and forced water vapor to condense out of the air. If the air outside is 65° and has as much water vapor as it can hold at that temperature, the weatherman says that the "relative humidity" is 100 per cent. But if the air has only half the water vapor it can hold at 65°, then the humidity is 50 per cent. Without water vapor in the air around us life would be strange. Many of our plants and trees would wither from the dry heat, there would be no rain, and the skies would be forever cloudless.

fog and clouds

Air temperature, water vapor, and the billions of dust particles floating in the air are responsible for that troublesome stuff we call fog. Air that is heavy with moisture is an ideal fog producer. As the air cools it is forced to give up some of its water vapor, which condenses on the billions of tiny dust particles in the air. Around each grain of dust hangs a small water droplet which remains suspended as a fog particle until the air is again warmed so the water can change back into vapor.

If you have spent much time near a lake you have probably seen what the weatherman calls "advection fog." Night air cooled by the nearby woods flows out over the lake and mixes with warm moist air just above the water. As the lake's warm air is cooled, a thin blanket of fog forms and hangs over the water until the midmorning sun evaporates it.

Advection fog is formed in the early hours of the morning over lakes. Warm moist air rising from the lake mixes with cool air from the land. Water vapor condenses, produces fog.

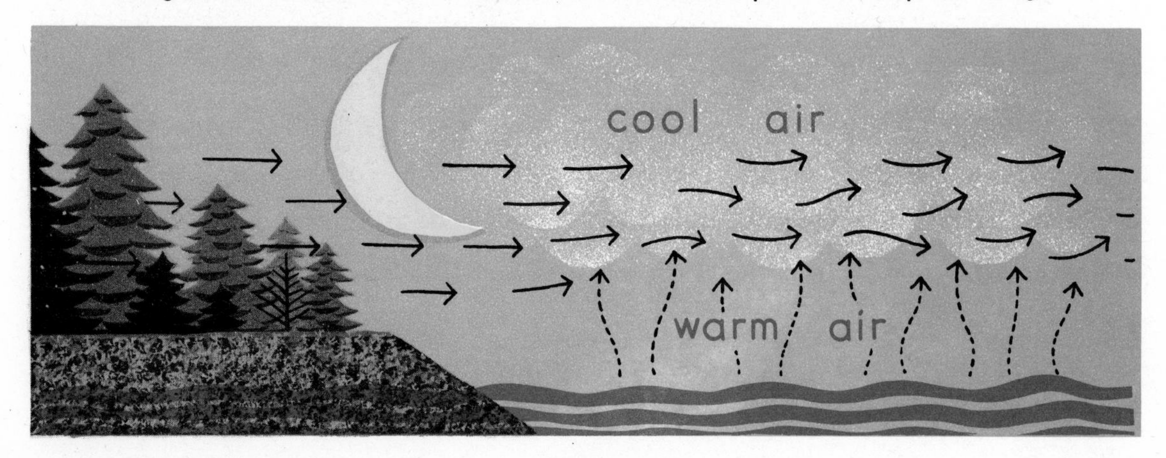

When smoke and soot from automobile exhausts and factory chimneys mix with fog, we call it "smog." On clear dry days when a wind is blowing, these bothersome particles are carried high into the air and are blown away. But on cool, damp days when there is no wind the particles hang low in the air. Industrial cities built in natural basins and in areas plagued by fog are the greatest smog centers, Los Angeles and Salt Lake City, for example. Perhaps London is most famous for smog. Because the British burn their coal wastefully, they release many millions of tons of smoke and coal gases into the air each year. Not only is it unpleasant for Londoners to breathe these fumes, it is also deadly. In one month, December 1952, thousands of Britishers were killed by smog. And in Donora, Pennsylvania, smog is said to have killed 20 people in one week and to have made hundreds of others ill.

Once you understand what makes fog, you know what a cloud is. When fog forms high in the sky we say that there are clouds. Or looking at it the other way, when clouds hang close to the ground we say that it is foggy.

Clouds are born when warm, moist air rises and is cooled. Sometimes water vapor condenses on dust particles to form a water-droplet cloud. Other times, when the water vapor is cold enough, a cloud of ice crystals is formed. On any cold winter day you can easily make your own cloud simply by exhaling into the air. People who have spent much time at sea know that clouds in the distance usually mean land. Hot moist air rising from an island is cooled aloft, and its water vapor condenses to form a cloud.

A boiling kettle will give you a private steam cloud. Hot, moist air inside escapes through the spout and is cooled by air around the stove. Water vapor condenses on the ceiling.

If you have spent any time at sea you know that clouds in the distance usually mean that land is nearby. Moist air which rises from an island cools, condenses to form a cloud.

Clouds come in many different shapes and sizes. On an overcast day the clouds form a solid blanket overhead. On other days you see small puffs of clouds which in the next moment may disappear. Weathermen the world over have agreed to give certain kinds of clouds certain names. Also, they know that rain and hot or cold weather can be predicted when clouds are read properly and associated with other weather elements.

CUMULUS—These are the fluffy, dome-shaped clouds with a gray, flat base. Sometimes you see them scattered across the sky at about 1600 feet. These clouds often ride atop currents of rising warm air. Most frequently you see cumulus clouds on summer days. They form in the morning and by evening they may be gone.

STRATO-CUMULUS—Patches of white or gray rounded clouds packed closely together so that their edges are touching. Sometimes they form an unbroken ceiling. The bases of these clouds are never higher than 6500 feet.

ALTO-CUMULUS—These look much the same as strato-cumulus clouds. Frequently they parade across the sky at different heights, in bands or in patches. Their edges are very thin and they are seen from 6000 to 20,000 feet up.

CIRRO-CUMULUS—These clouds form between 10,000 and 30,000 feet. They are small and fluffy, have no shading, and arrange themselves

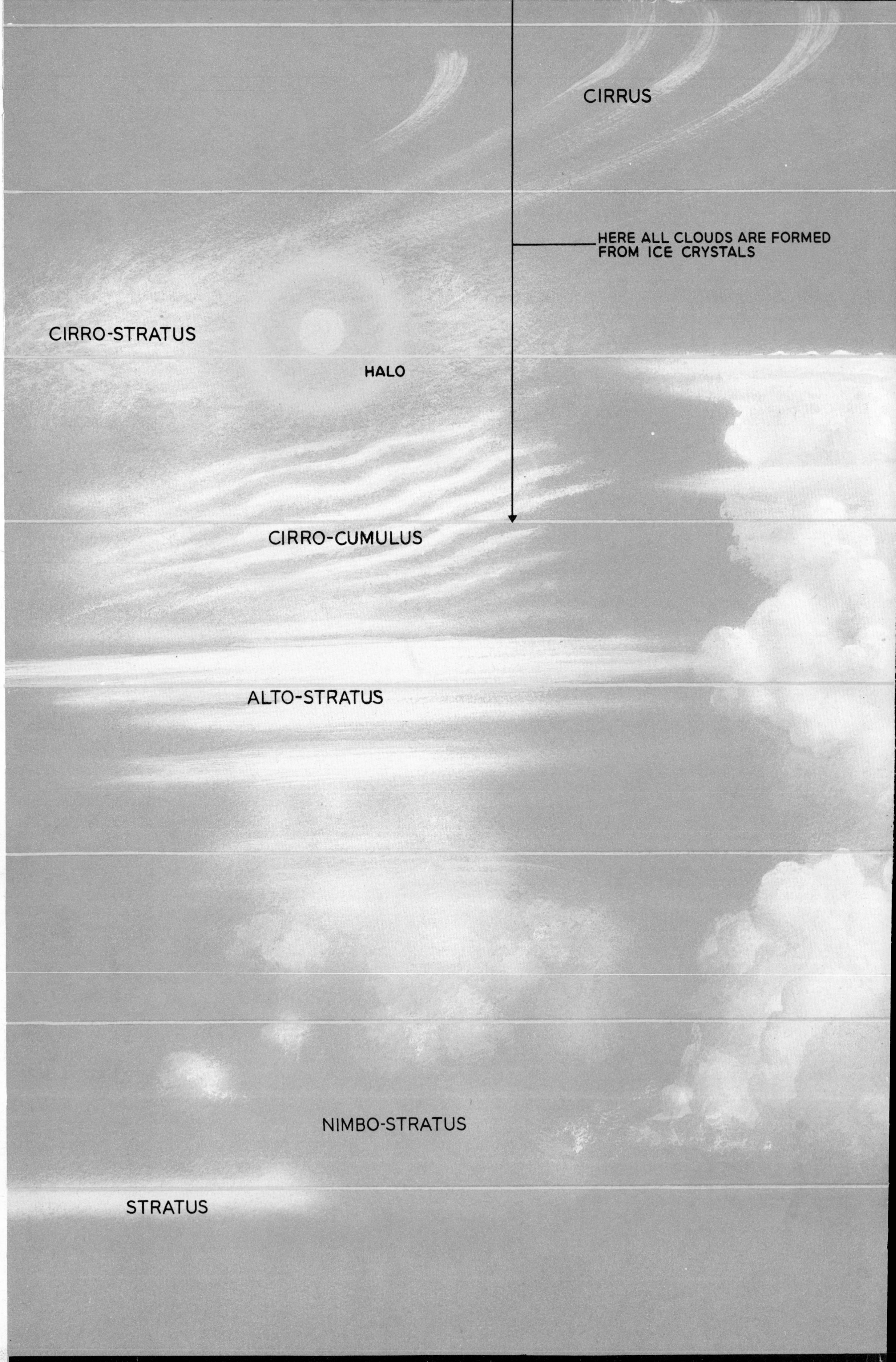

CIRRUS

HERE ALL CLOUDS ARE FORMED FROM ICE CRYSTALS

CIRRO-STRATUS

HALO

CIRRO-CUMULUS

ALTO-STRATUS

NIMBO-STRATUS

STRATUS

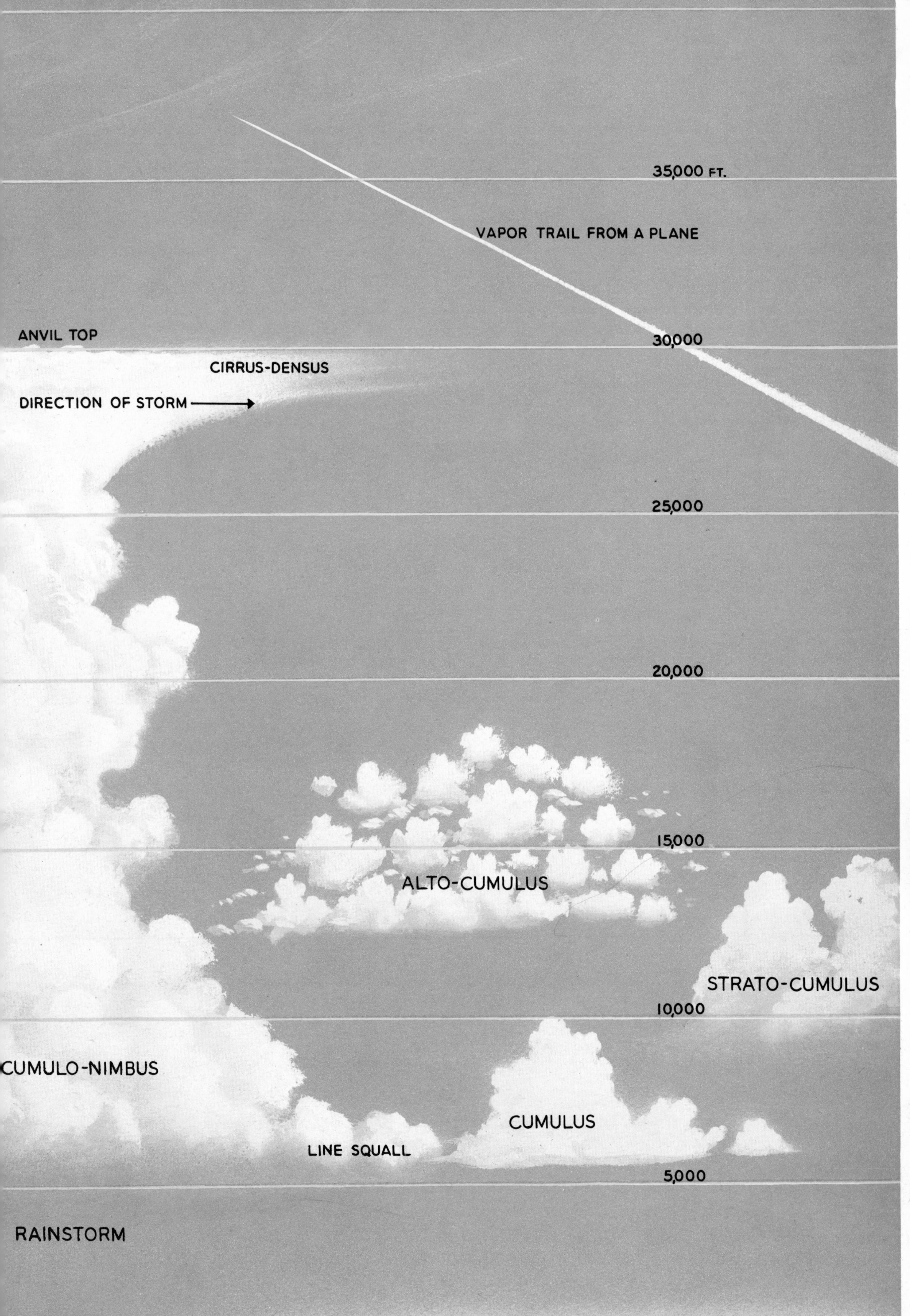
35,000 FT.
VAPOR TRAIL FROM A PLANE
ANVIL TOP
30,000
CIRRUS-DENSUS
DIRECTION OF STORM
25,000
20,000
15,000
ALTO-CUMULUS
STRATO-CUMULUS
10,000
CUMULO-NIMBUS
CUMULUS
LINE SQUALL
5,000
RAINSTORM
FOG

in ripples like blown desert sand. These are the clouds we see when we say there is a "mackerel sky."

CUMULO-NIMBUS—Violent summer thunderstorms showering hail often come from these massive and towering clouds of the cumulus family. On a hot summer day you can watch them build as their tops restlessly boil higher and higher. Within these clouds there are violent up-and-down wind currents. A fully developed cumulo-nimbus has a thin anvil-shaped top of ice crystals which is stretched flat by high winds aloft.

STRATUS—Probably the least interesting of all clouds is the stratus, a thin foglike layer usually not more than 50 or 100 feet thick. Sometimes the sky above can be seen through these clouds. They hang from 1000 to 6000 feet above the ground.

NIMBO-STRATUS—These clouds are like stratus clouds, only they are often thicker and darker. Their bases are usually not higher than 3000 feet but are sometimes as low as 100 feet. Continuous spring rains and drizzles come from these clouds.

ALTO-STRATUS—The third member of the stratus family. These clouds are usually thick and dark gray or bluish layers between 6500 and 20,000 feet. Occasionally they are so thin that you can see the sun or moon dimly outlined through them.

CIRRO-STRATUS—These are high stratus clouds which stretch across the sky, producing a thin white veil. They are the clouds that create the "ring around the moon." When the sun shines through them it casts a shadow, but does not when it shines through alto-stratus clouds.

CIRRUS—The senior member of this family, because these clouds move near the top of the troposphere yet they can be as low as 10,000 feet. Caught by winds aloft, these thin, feathery clouds made of ice crystals race by at speeds of 100 to 200 miles an hour. But their great height gives us the impression that they are drifting slowly.

rain, sleet, hail, and snow

The water vapor, dust particles, and temperature of clouds combine and bring us rain, snow, sleet, and hail. One meteorologist has estimated that 4,000,000 (four million) gallons of water in these four forms

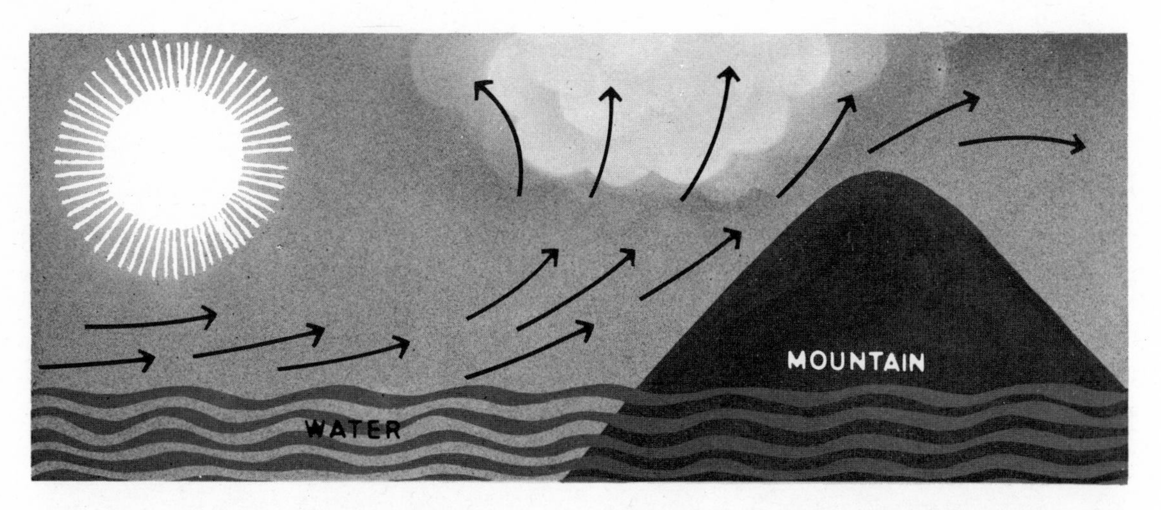

Air passing over oceans becomes heavy with moisture. As the air moves overland, it is pushed up the slopes of mountains. As it climbs it cools, its water vapor forms clouds.

pour down on the earth *every second.* While some areas of the world are overshowered, people in other regions consider themselves lucky if they get three good downpours a year. What does the weatherman consider an "average" rainfall? Well, New York City gets about 40 inches of rain a year, San Francisco about 20, Chicago about 30, and New Orleans about 50.

The wettest spot in the world is a place called Cherrapunji, India, perched nearly a mile above sea level in the Khasi mountain range. It rains there most of the year. Hot moist air from the Indian Ocean flows steadily overland and climbs the mountains. As this moist air is pushed higher and higher by the continuous flow of more air behind, it cools and rain pours down on the people below. The yearly rainfall for Cherrapunji averages 450 inches. In one 4-day period 100 inches of rain fell. In 1861 the people of Cherrapunji sloshed through 905 inches of rain. Compare this with the driest spot in the United States, Greenland Ranch, Death Valley, which has an average yearly rainfall of less than 1.5 inches! An imaginative New York *Times* reporter once had this to say about the Cherrapunji rainy season: ". . . The rain comes down in drops the size of baseballs, blown by the fierce winds with rifle velocity. . . ."

A typical rain cloud has billions upon billions of tiny water droplets which are buffeted about within the cloud. As they collide, some of them grow larger and larger. When these drops are heavy enough so they can no longer be supported by drafts and winds in the cloud, gravity pulls them to the earth. It rains. But sometimes the air below a raining cloud is so dry that the raindrops evaporate before they can reach the ground.

England, whose air is constantly kept damp by moist winds blowing in from the Atlantic, is an ideal rain-making area. Even if a bright sun is shining in the morning, the Englishman hooks his umbrella on his arm before leaving for work. And sure enough, by lunch time he may have cause to use it.

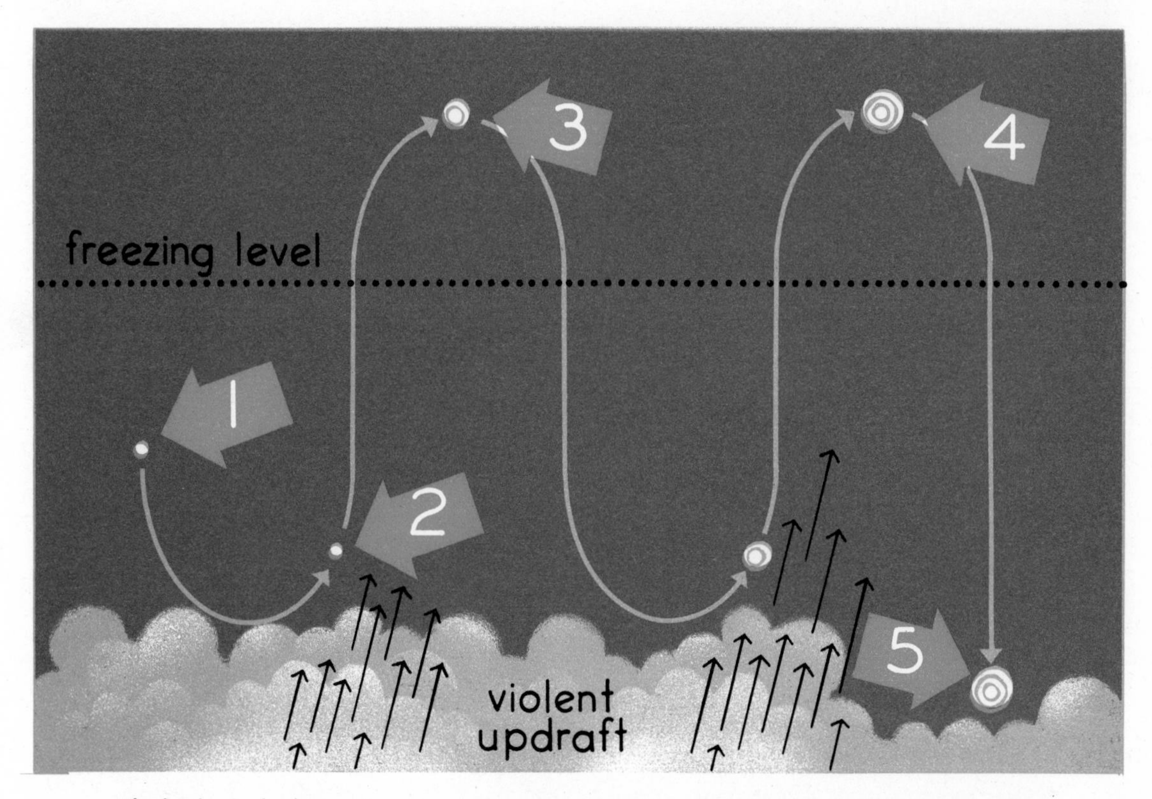

The birth of a hailstone: Frozen raindrops are sometimes turned into hail as shown here. First a raindrop is lifted to the cold region of a cloud by updrafts. When it freezes it begins to drop out of the cloud but is again shot aloft, each time acquiring a new shell of water, which freezes. Eventually the hailstone becomes heavy enough to fall out of the cloud.

In damp climates during the winter months rain sometimes freezes and falls as sleet. If it manages to reach the ground without freezing, but turns to ice when it strikes trees, telephone wires, and the highways, we call it glaze.

If there are strong wind currents in a cloud, frozen rain is turned into hail. The winds catch the small pellets of ice and bounce them around. As a pellet begins to fall out of the cloud it is caught by an updraft and lifted to the cold top region of the cloud. The film of water covering the pellet is frozen and it falls again. But a second time it is blown to the top of the cloud where it collects another coat of ice, and still another, until it becomes so heavy that the winds can no longer hold it. At this point it falls to earth as a hailstone.

The next time you are in a hailstorm cut a hailstone in half to see how it is made. You'll notice that, like an onion, it is composed of several layers. By counting the layers you can tell exactly how many trips the hailstone made to the top of the cloud before it fell to earth. The stronger the wind within a hail cloud, the larger the hailstones will be. How large can a hailstone get? The largest one on record weighed 1.5 pounds and measured more than 5 inches across. It fell at Potter, Nebraska, July 6, 1928.

Unlike hailstones and raindrops, a snowflake undergoes what the meteorologist calls "sublimation." The water vapor turns into ice crystals without first becoming a raindrop. Some meteorologists think that all of our rain may begin as snowflakes that melt when they fall through warm air. But like other frontiers of weather research, the forces that create a raindrop are still pretty much of a mystery.

Now that we have seen how nature manufactures some of the products that bring us different kinds of weather, let's look at that weather in action.

hurricanes, tornadoes, and thunderstorms

hurricanes

The hurricane is the most destructive storm known to man. Along a path hundreds of miles long a full-scale hurricane can kill thousands of people, and damage property amounting to millions of dollars.

The forces making up a hurricane are raging winds, lashing rains, and angry seas. In 1932 hurricane seas washed 2500 people to their death in Cuba. Another of these storms killed 300,000 people in the Bay of Bengal. The only favorable thing that can be said for the hurricane is that it very quickly makes man realize how small and powerless he is in comparison with nature on a rampage.

Hurricanes are known by several names. Pacific-island people call them typhoons. In Australia they are known as willy-willies. And around the Indian Ocean they are called cyclones.

All hurricanes are born over the ocean near the equator, in that area called the doldrums. For days and weeks the blistering sun beats down on the calm ocean water. Slowly the air above the sea becomes heated and begins to spiral lazily overhead. More hot moist air rushes in toward the spiral and is drawn skyward. Gradually this circle of twisting air grows larger, spinning faster and faster counterclockwise. As the hot

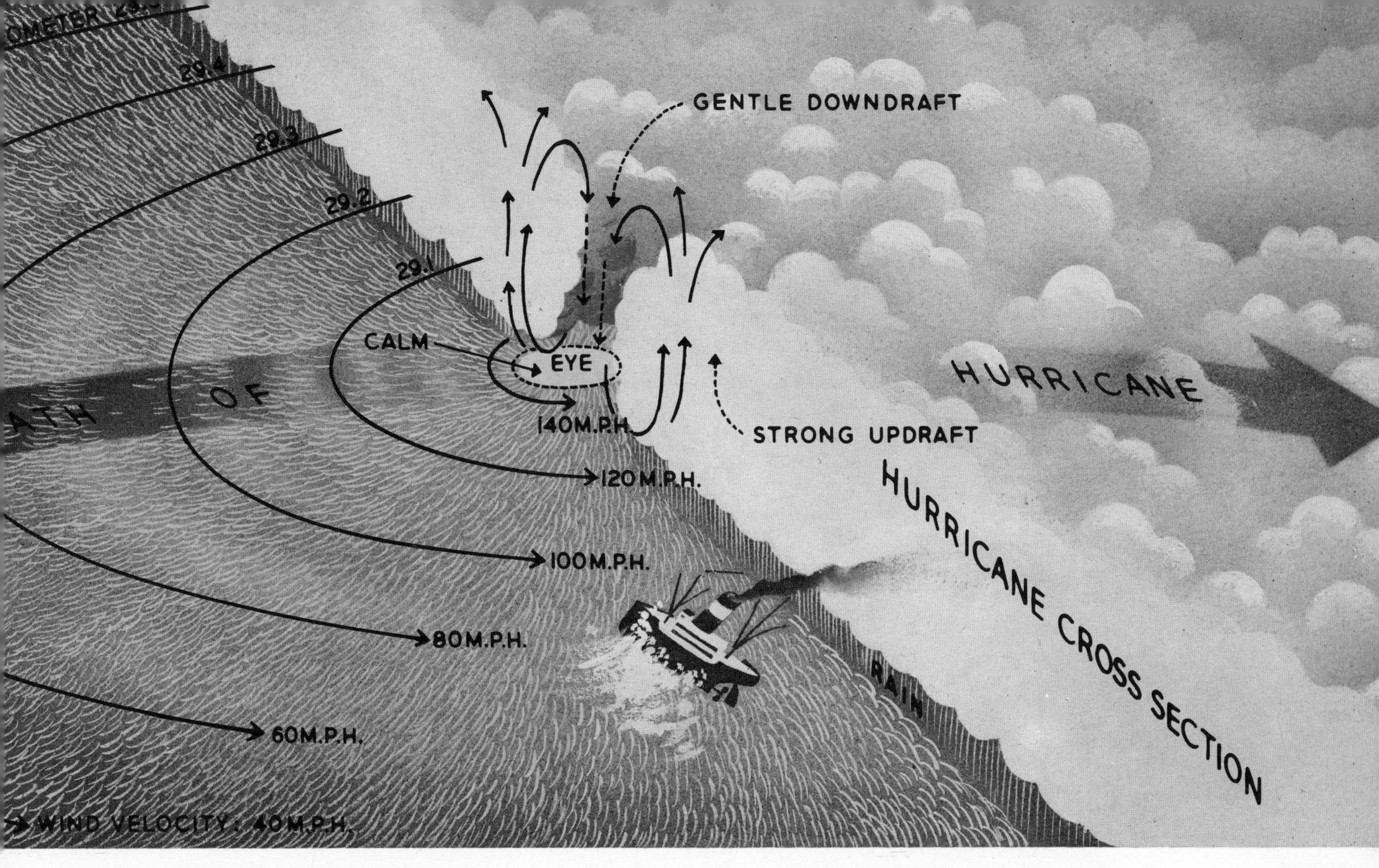

In a hurricane the winds circle counterclockwise around the "eye" center, about fifteen miles in width.

moist air around the top of the spiral is cooled, great rain clouds are formed. With a near limitless "fuel" supply of hot moist air below the circling winds, rain and clouds grow in their fury. Inside the spiral is a circle of calm known as the hurricane's "eye." Directly overhead there are often clear blue skies, but around the rim rain and winds of 150 to 200 miles an hour rage. The eye of a full-blown hurricane averages 15 miles across. The clouds marking the width of the storm may cover an area 600 miles across. If you have ever been in a hurricane, you are well aware of the fierce rains. In 1911 a severe hurricane which struck Luzon in the Philippines dropped nearly 4 feet of water in 24 hours!

Once a hurricane is on the warpath and heads toward land, it sends out several warnings for the weatherman to read. One of these is unusually high tides. Others are a falling barometer, which shows an advancing low-pressure area, cirro-stratus clouds producing a ring around the moon, then alto-stratus, and finally alto-cumulus clouds.

If weathermen are able to read these warning signs quickly enough, they try to predict the path of the hurricane and warn people in the way. But hurricanes are like women, you can never be sure just what they're going to do next. (Maybe this is why hurricanes are given women's names, such as Carol, Louise, and Barbara.) If the weatherman isn't in a position to read the warning signs soon enough, or if the storm suddenly changes its course, then we have full-scale destruction like that brought by the famous New England hurricane of 1938.

This storm snaked its way around Florida, up the coast, and seemed to be moving north "fairly well off the Atlantic seaboard," thought the Weather Bureau. But then two unexpected things happened. Suddenly it changed its course and headed straight for Long Island and New England. And it stepped up its speed from 30 miles an hour to 50 and 60 miles an hour. Then it struck.

Long Island was pounded by tidal waves 3 and 4 stories high. The beaches were swept clean of boats, sheds, and everything that wasn't bolted or lashed down. In the town of Westhampton Beach 144 buildings were wrecked. Only 6 remained standing. Scores of people were drowned. The storm raged north, leaving death and ruin everywhere. When it reached Providence, Rhode Island, it sent a 12-foot tidal wave across the city. Water washed over the tops of streetcars and automobiles. People were drowning in hotel lobbies. In Rhode Island alone 494 people were killed; 4500 buildings were ruined and 15,139 damaged. When the storm reached Boston, Massachusetts, Harvard's Blue Hill Observatory recorded winds of 187 miles an hour for five minutes. The next day the storm blew itself out, near Ottawa, Canada. It had spent itself by traveling overland and eventually running out of "fuel."

With the passing of the storm, man began to count the damage. Thousands of people saw their homes swept away. The number dead was more than 650. Damage to property was $400,000,000 (four hundred million dollars). One meteorologist called the storm the "costliest" natural disaster we have ever known.

tornadoes

A close relative of the hurricane is the tornado, that black weaving vacuum funnel that can suck animals, automobiles, and even houses up into its hungry snout. Like most weather the tornado is caused by a clash of moist warm air with cold dry air. The tornado belt in the United States is in the Missouri-Mississippi Basin. On hot summer days people in this region grow anxious when the skies darken and they sense

a thunderstorm in the making. Warm moist air flows into this area from the Gulf of Mexico and the Caribbean. At the same time cold dry air passing over the Rockies settles on top of the warm air. Where their surfaces touch, rainclouds begin to boil and a storm is born. The warm air below sets up a spinning action around a hollow center. As the spiral whips around faster a tornado is made.

Its deadly funnel zigzags across the ground. Winds sweeping around the funnel reach speeds of 300 miles an hour or more. And within the funnel are sucking winds of 100 to 200 miles an hour. Like a giant vacuum cleaner, the funnel wanders overland at 25 to 40 miles an hour, drawing into its snout nearly everything it strikes. When it passes over a building the building usually explodes. Tightly packed air inside the building expands so rapidly that it pushes the walls out in all directions and blows the roof off. The splinters of lumber left are then sucked up into the tornado's funnel and are carried off.

Unlike a hurricane, a tornado sweeps over an extremely narrow track of land. The distance across the business end of a tornado is seldom more than 1000 feet and these storms usually peter out after traveling a few miles. One of the things that makes them terrifying is that you can never be sure where they are going. For a while one may boom along in a straight path, suddenly it zigzags off to the left, then weaves back to the right. People watching a tornado can only hope that the funnel will not sweep over them.

One of the most vivid descriptions of a tornado ever written appeared in the magazine *Monthly Weather Review,* May 1930. It was written by Will Keller, a Greenburg, Kansas, farmer who lived through one of these ferocious storms.

"At last the great shaggy end of the funnel hung directly overhead. Everything was as still as death. There was a strong gassy odor, and it seemed as though I could not breathe. There was a screaming, hissing sound coming directly from the end of the funnel. I looked up, and to my astonishment saw right into the heart of the tornado. There was a circular opening in the center of the funnel about 50 to 100 feet in diameter, and extending straight upward for a distance of at least half a mile. . . . The walls . . . were rotating clouds and the hole was brilliantly lighted with constant flashes of lightning which zigzagged from side to side.

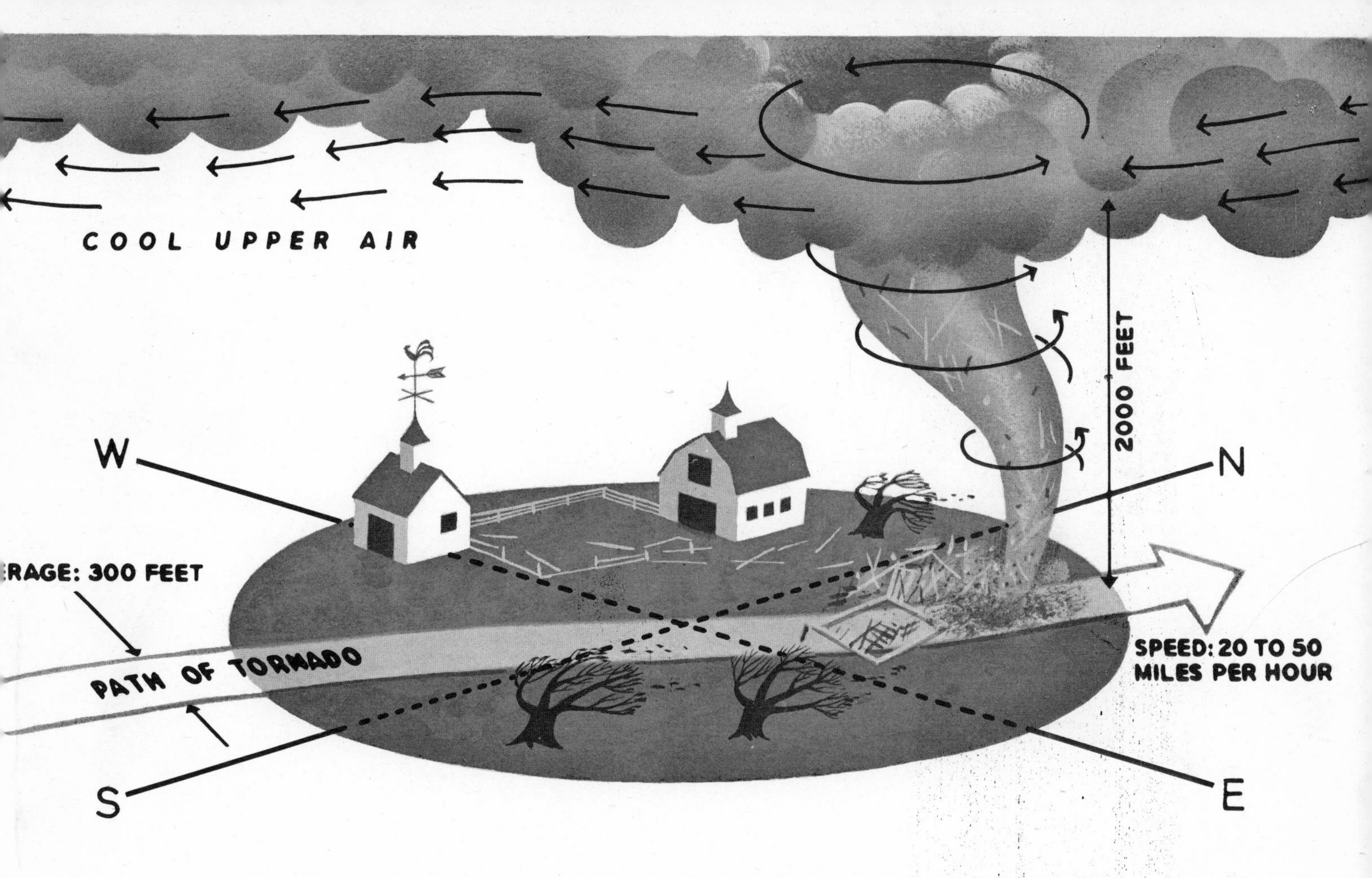

The winds in a tornado's funnel reach speeds of three hundred miles an hour or more.

"Around the rim of the great vortex, small tornadoes were constantly forming and breaking away. These looked like tails as they writhed their way around the funnel. It was these that made the hissing sound. . . .

"The tornado was not traveling at a great speed. I had plenty of time to get a good view of the whole thing, inside and out. . . .

"After it passed my place it again dipped and struck and demolished the house and barn of a farmer by the name of Evans. . . . Not having time to reach their cellar, they took refuge under a small bluff that faced to the leeward of the approaching tornado. They lay down flat on the ground and caught hold of some plum bushes which fortunately grew within their reach. As it was, they felt themselves lifted from the ground. Mr. Evans said that he could see the wreckage of his house, among it being the cook stove going round and round over his head. . . ."

thunderstorms

At least once during the summer you can count on being caught in a thunderstorm. The most reliable sign of these storms is the majestic

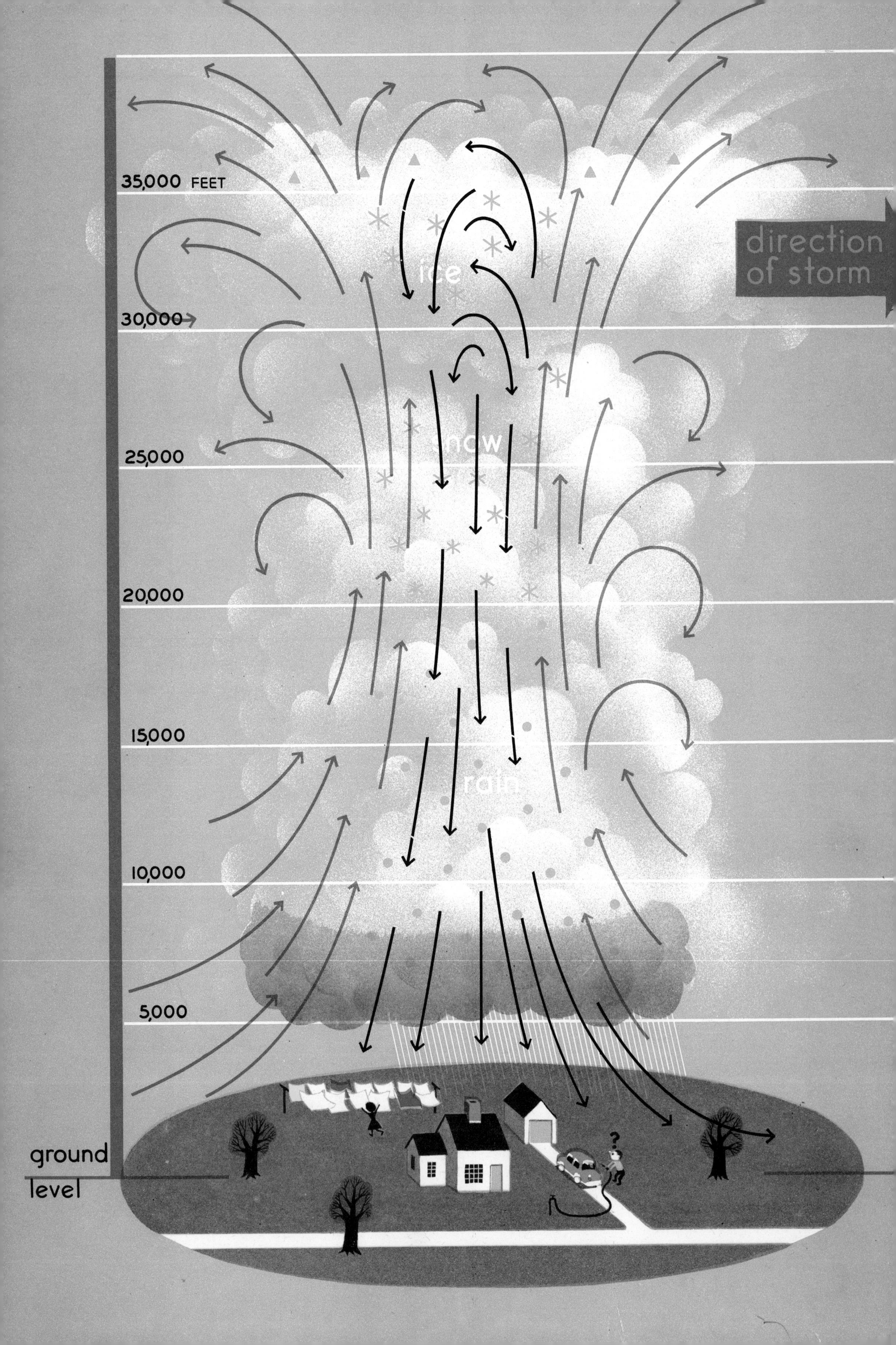
35,000 FEET
30,000
25,000
20,000
15,000
10,000
5,000
ground
level
ice
snow
rain
direction
of storm
?

thunderhead cloud, the cumulo-nimbus. The afternoon may be clear and hot with the sun beating down on a nearby field. But a storm is in the making. The heat from the field causes the moist hot air over it to rise. When it reaches cooling heights, water vapor in the air condenses out and a cloud is formed. If the rising moist air currents are strong enough, the air will continue to push higher and higher to cirrus levels where the water vapor is turned into ice crystals. As the cloud builds, water vapor condenses into rain and the storm officially begins, flashing lightning and booming thunder. At the top of the cloud there may be hail, snow, and sleet, but it seldom reaches the ground. Warmer parts of the cloud and hot air below melt the ice and snow before they can fall to the ground.

Meteorologists are not sure how lightning in a thunderstorm is made. They think the sharp updrafts, downdrafts, and crosscurrents within a cloud cause the cloud's particles to rub against each other so vigorously that electrical charges are set up. You can set up an electrical charge of your own by scuffing your feet across the living-room rug. If you then touch your finger to a brass doorknob you'll see a spark and get a shock. This is what happens when lightning strikes, only there is a lot more action. If a negatively charged cloud passes over positively charged ground, the cloud releases a bolt of electrons which strike as lightning. Lightning can also strike from ground to cloud, from cloud to cloud, and even within a single cloud.

The thunderclap you hear after a lightning flash is created by rapidly heated air which expands when lightning streaks through it. And the distant rumbling is caused by the thunder's sound waves bouncing back and forth within clouds or between mountains.

air masses

For four chapters we have been talking about "moist warm" and "cold dry" masses of air that roam over oceans and continents as though they were created by magic. Each air mass that brings us a heat wave or a cold wave has a beginning. The weatherman calls the breeding grounds of air masses "source regions." Throughout the world there are about twenty source regions which day and night are manufacturing air masses for export. But we will take up only three of them which have a major

←Motion of air within a storm cloud

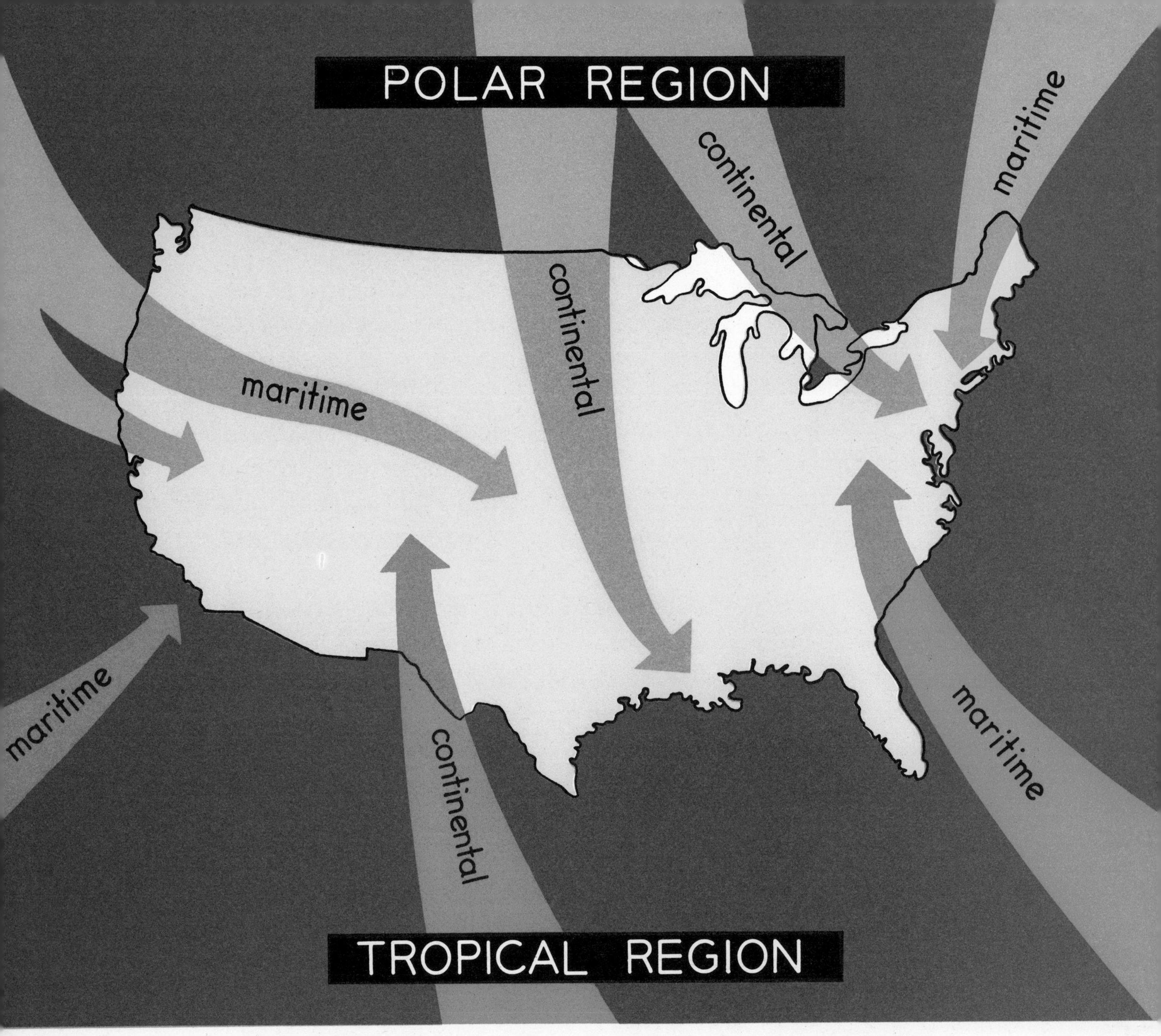

There are about twenty "source regions," or breeding grounds for air masses. Those that form over the sea are called maritime masses. Continental masses form over land areas.

influence on the weather which we experience in the United States.

CONTINENTAL POLAR—From Labrador to the Rockies and from southern Canada to the Arctic Circle is a broad area of land that becomes extremely cold in winter. Air hanging over this region day by day grows colder, at times reaching a low of 50° below zero. Eventually this great mass of air moves south and east down over the United States. In one day it may move 500 miles. As it flows steadily over mountains and across plains its lower levels are warmed slightly by the land. But it is still cold enough so the weatherman warns us that we're in for a February cold wave that may last four or five days. These continental-polar

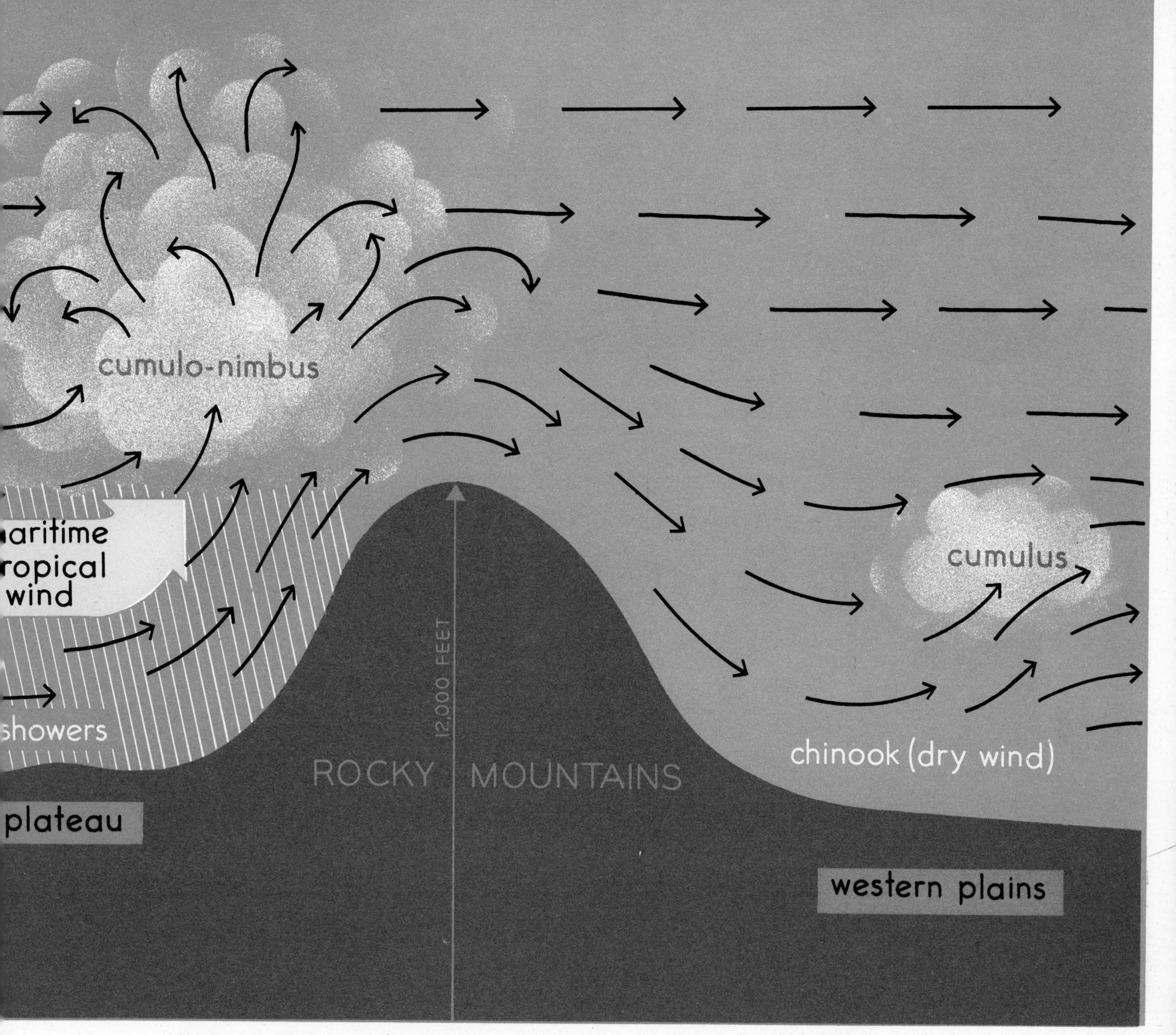

Moisture in rising air condenses out as rain. Dry down-mountain air is called Chinook.

cold air masses sometimes reach as far south as Florida and chill tourists who have gone there for a two-week vacation away from winter. We can always rely on cold waves (or summer "cool waves") from Canada to bring us dry weather and crystal clear skies.

MARITIME POLAR—This air mass has its source region over the sea. It flows in a southeast direction, picking up large amounts of moisture as it crosses the North Pacific. People on the West Coast are most familiar with this air mass.

In winter it strikes the coast as warm air laden with moisture. As it climbs its first barricade, California's Cascade Range, it cools and releases showers on the people below. But high in the mountains the water vapor is turned into snow which often blocks roads for days at a time. Having lost most of its moisture, the dry air next plunges down the other side of the Cascades, growing warm as it descends. This dry down-the-mountain wind is called a "chinook," or the snow-eater, because it absorbs great quantities of ground and air moisture.

Continuing its journey, the air mass next crosses the Sierras and the Rockies, each time losing more of its moisture. In modified form it moves across the Great Plains, struggles over the Appalachians, and finally slips meekly out over the Atlantic Ocean.

MARITIME TROPICAL—The Gulf of Mexico, Sargasso and Caribbean seas form the breeding grounds for maritime-tropical air masses. For days and weeks at a time the sun beats down on this area, heating and moistening the air until it starts on its journey northeast across a major section of the United States. But it seldom moves far enough west to cross the Rockies. In summer maritime-tropical air masses bring us hot sticky weather with poor visibility. Thermal currents push this air aloft, creating cumulus and cumulo-nimbus clouds which burst into thunderstorms in the afternoons. In winter warm and moist maritime air mixes with air cooled by the land; the result is fog and calm gray days overcast with cheerless stratus clouds.

fronts

The weatherman would have an easy time of predicting the weather if air masses moved over the country one at a time. But weather life is not so simple. All it takes is for two different air masses to collide and we have weather action.

COLD FRONTS—Imagine for a moment that a great mass of hot moist air from the Gulf of Mexico has settled over the eastern section of the United States. People in Memphis, Washington, D.C., New York, and Boston complain about the warm and sticky weather. Then they read the weather page in their newspapers and learn that a mass of cold dry air is sweeping down from Canada. Relief is in sight.

In the shape of a shallow bowl turned upside down, the cold air mass advances at 20 miles an hour and covers an area 1000 miles wide and about 10 miles high. It bears down on the hot air mass and runs into it. Because cold air is heavier than warm air, the cold air mass rides along the ground, nosing its way forward under the warm air like a wedge. So all along a gentle slope from ground to sky the two air masses touch. And where their surfaces meet is called a "front," in this case a cold front because the cold air mass is pushing the warm air out of the way.

There are definite weather changes you can expect when a cold front passes by. Near the ground, along the leading edge of the front, you can expect mist or fog, created when the warm moist air is cooled. Higher along the front's surface, swelling cumulo-nimbus clouds form rapidly and release heavy showers. These are caused by the warm moist air being pushed aloft and cooling. The mixture of warm and cool air along the front may also bring strong winds. (The greater the difference in temperature and humidity of the two air masses, the more violent frontal weather will be.) Still higher along the front are alto-cumulus and cumulus clouds which thin out and eventually disappear. These last clouds mark the tail end of the front and indicate that the cold air mass has moved in.

The cold front may continue its way across the country and move out over the Atlantic Ocean, or it may stop and settle over the eastern part of the country. Suppose it does the latter, let's see what kind of weather we would have if a warm front edged its way toward the cold air mass.

WARM FRONTS—The warm moist air working its way up from the Gulf of Mexico is lighter than the cold air mass. Because it is lighter when it meets the cold air it rides up a long slope.

Unlike the advancing cold front, the warm front first shows itself at high altitudes. Warm air at the top of the slope gives birth to the feathery cirrus clouds made of ice crystals. Lower down the slope, as the front begins to pass overhead, are cirro-stratus or alto-stratus clouds which close in and threaten rain. Still lower along the front dark nimbo-stratus clouds form and bring a steady rain. At the last stages of the front these clouds may droop so low that we are enclosed in fog. But when the front finally passes, the weather clears and we find ourselves damp and warm, already looking forward to more of that cool dry Canadian air to rescue us.

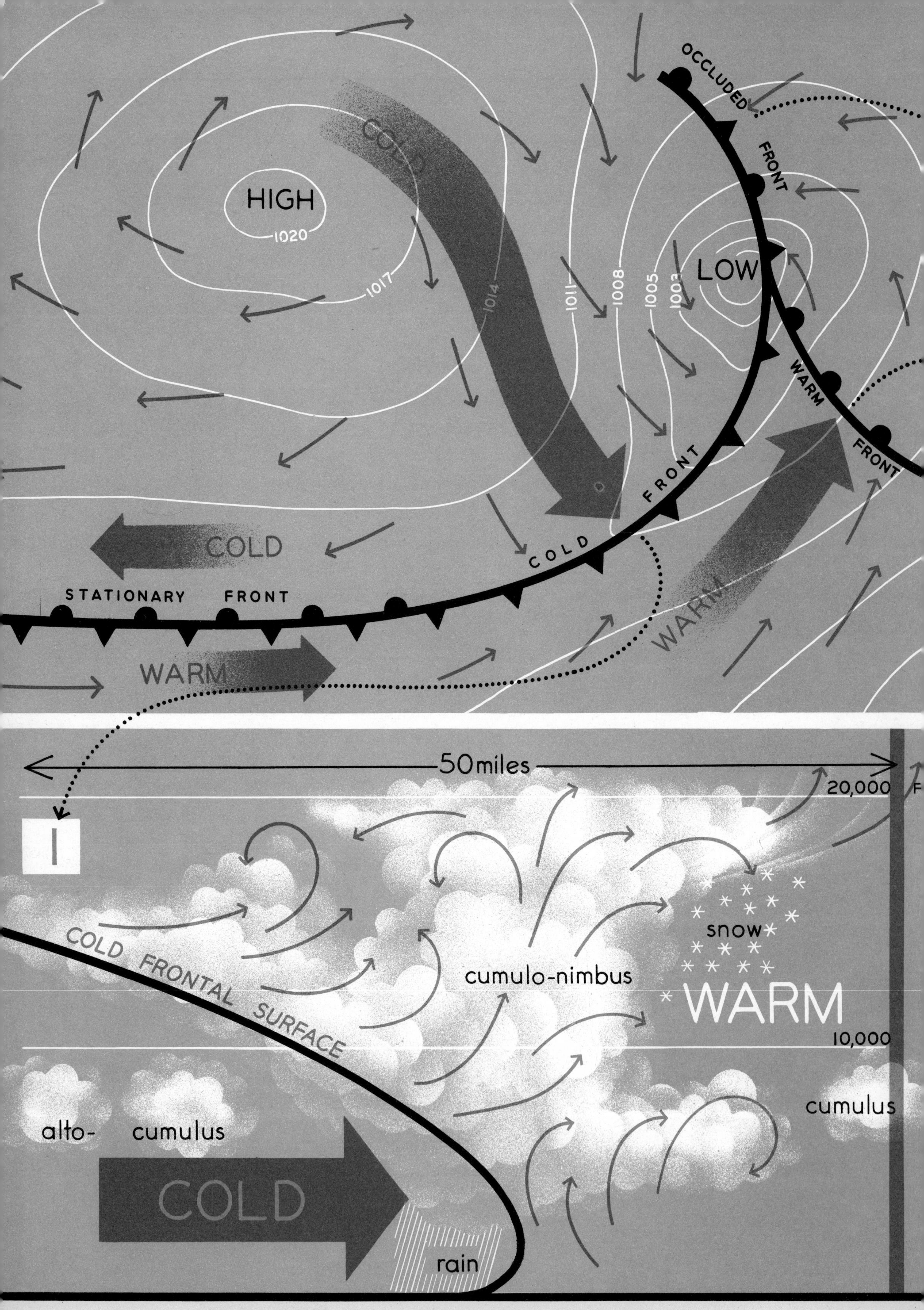

Top left drawing shows a typical weather picture which you might see in your daily newspaper. Fronts, motion of air, and pressure readings are indicated. Panel 1 shows a cross section of an advancing cold front accompanied by typical frontal clouds, rain and other weather. Signs of a cold front may be rain, lifting clouds, then clearing and dry weather.

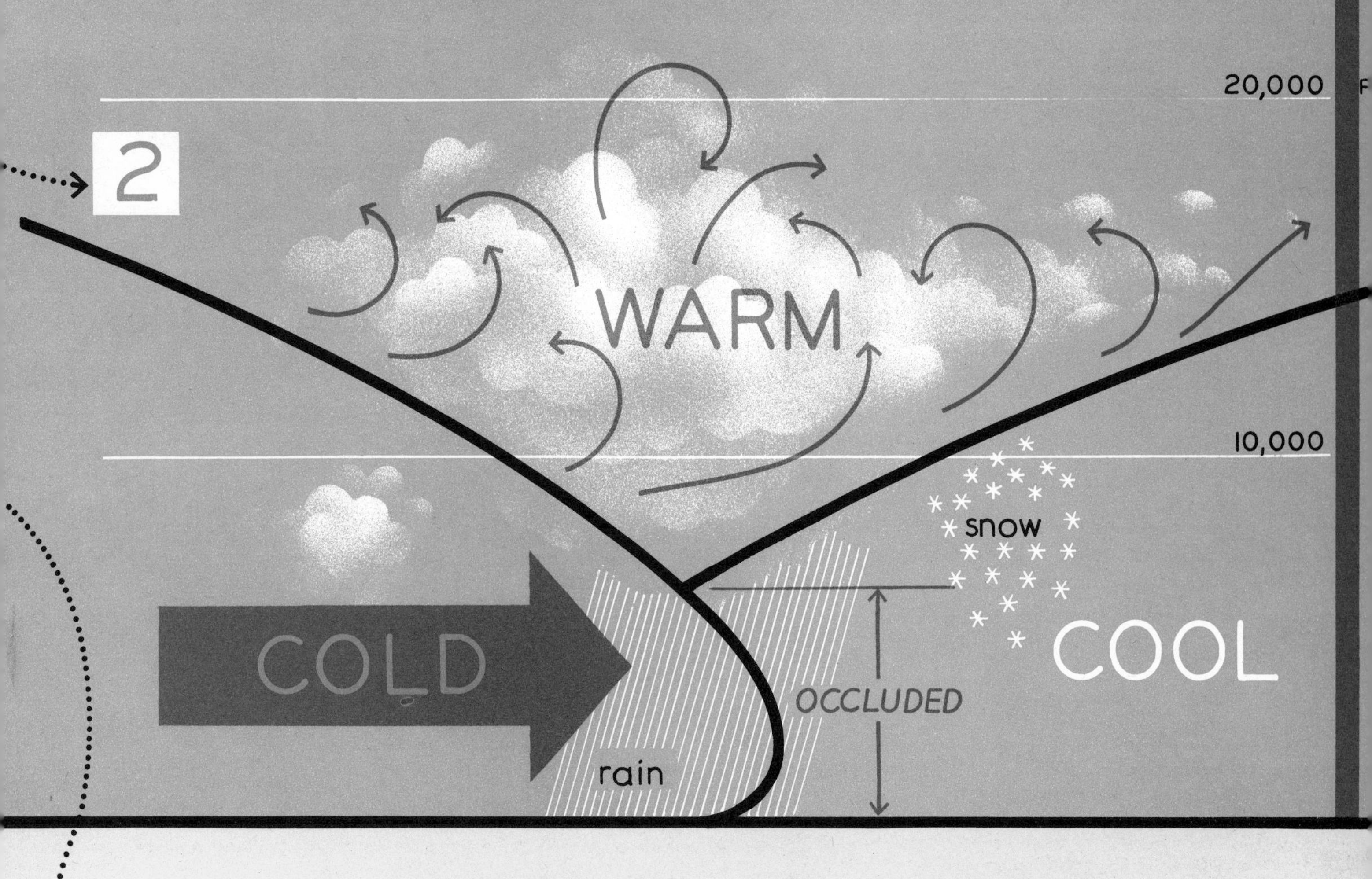

When one cold front overtakes one ahead and when warm air is sandwiched between the two, an occluded front is produced as shown here. Warm air is forced up, creates rain.

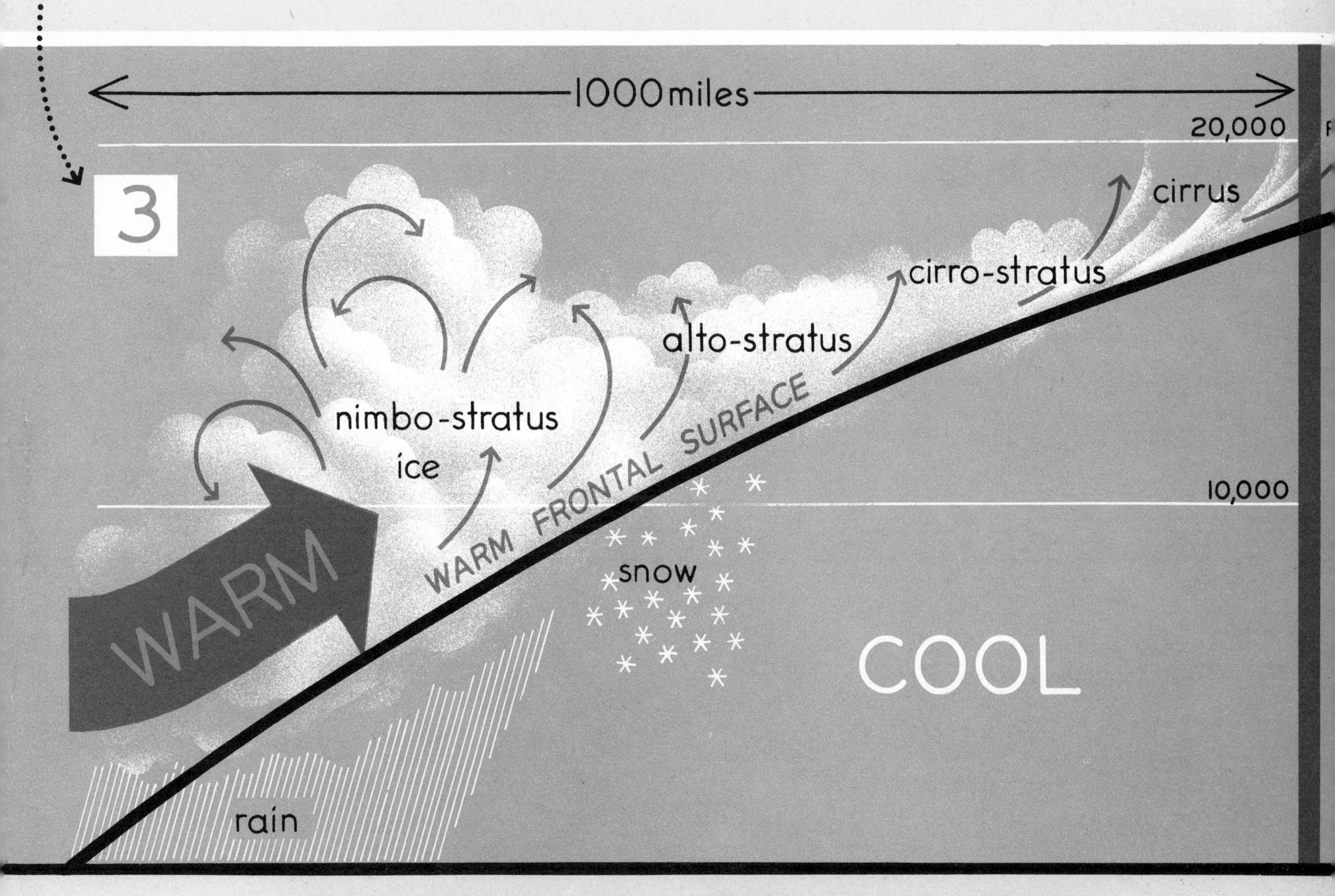

When a warm front overtakes a cold front, it slowly climbs up the slanting rear edge of the cold front. The warm front announces its approach with high thin clouds. Gradually other clouds begin forming at lower levels. Soon the sky is solid cloud and the rains begin to shower down. Re-examine the three panels and forecast the weather that fronts bring.

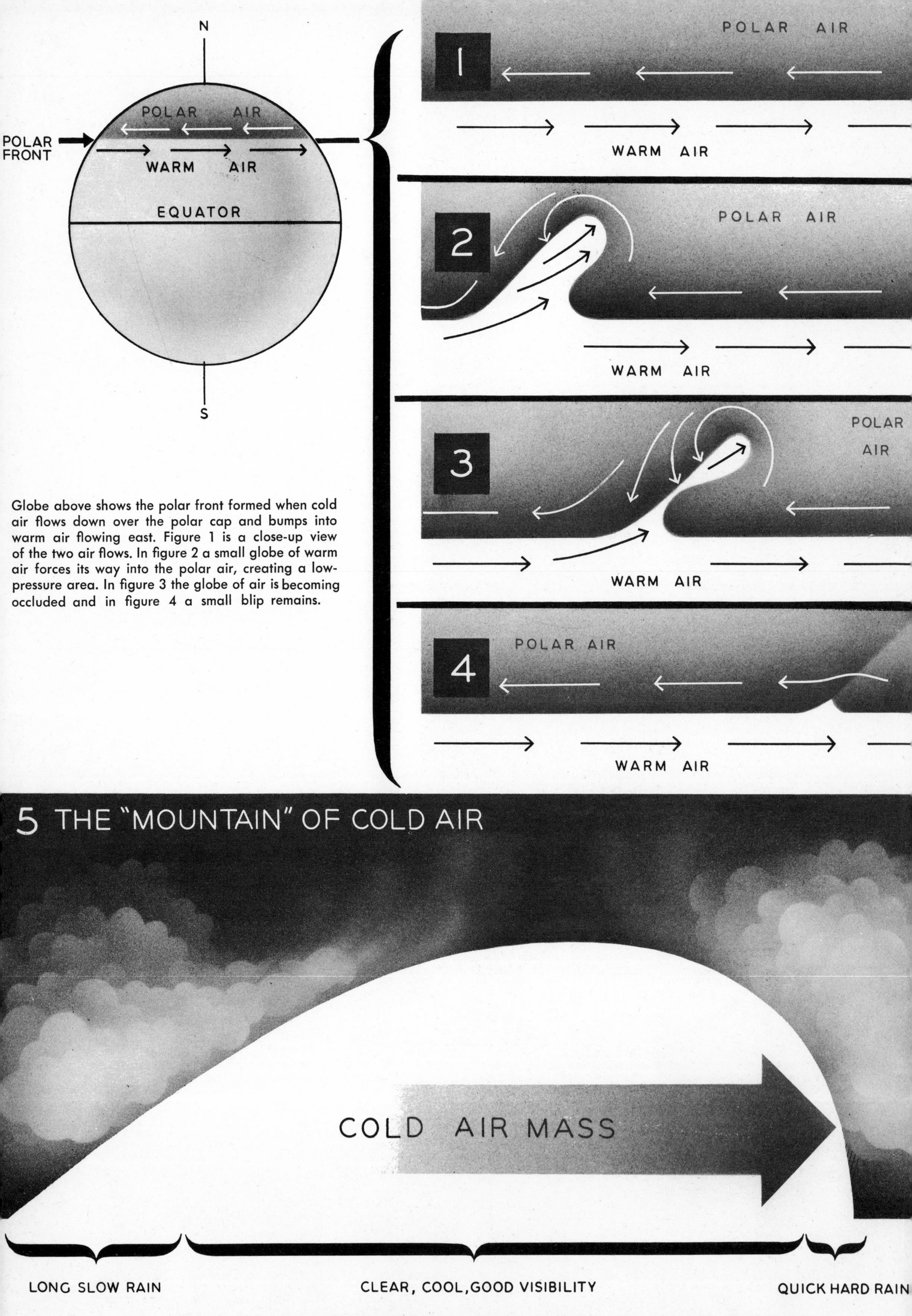

Globe above shows the polar front formed when cold air flows down over the polar cap and bumps into warm air flowing east. Figure 1 is a close-up view of the two air flows. In figure 2 a small globe of warm air forces its way into the polar air, creating a low-pressure area. In figure 3 the globe of air is becoming occluded and in figure 4 a small blip remains.

Figure 5 shows a large air mass which has become cooled. As its leading edge advances, typical cold-front weather occurs along the front. And along its trailing edge typical warm-front weather occurs.

tomorrow's weather

Warm fronts, continental-polar air masses, cumulo-nimbus clouds, temperature, and the many other weather signs are the weatherman's bread and butter. By learning what these signs mean he is able to tell us what kind of weather to expect tomorrow and next week. The forecasts you see on television, in your newspaper, and hear on the radio come from your nearest Weather Bureau office. After recording local weather conditions—temperature, wind direction and speed, humidity, cloud types, and so on—the forecaster nearest you enters this information on his weather map and announces tomorrow's weather. The map he works with is new each day, and each hour for that matter. This daily map shows a general picture of weather all over the country. To produce this picture more than 400 meteorologists from coast to coast take samples of the weather at certain times each day.

By reading these maps in your newspaper for a few days you'll be able to follow the weather as it moves across the country from west to east. And with a little practice you should be able to do your own weather predicting, to some degree, by keeping close track of the movement of air masses and fronts.

READING A WEATHER MAP:

1

WEATHER PATTERNS MOVE FROM WEST TO EAST ABOUT 500 MILES PER DAY, FASTER IN THE WINTER.

2

COLD
WARM

HIGH (COLD AIR) TRAVELS FASTER THAN THE LOW (W
AIR). BOTH FOLLOW THE GENERAL PATHS SHOWN HE

MAP OF A KIND THAT MAY APPEAR IN LOCAL NEWSPAPERS

3

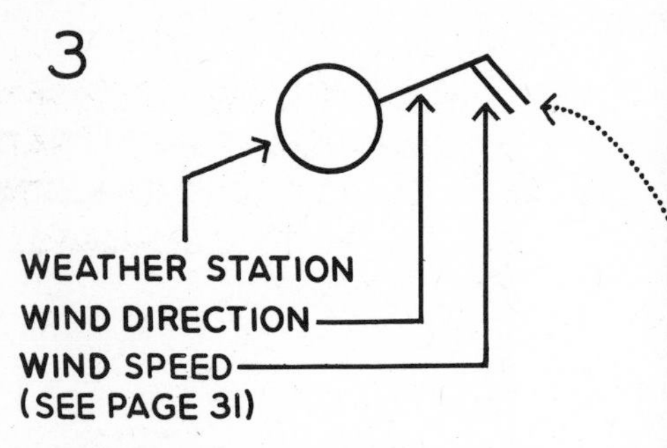

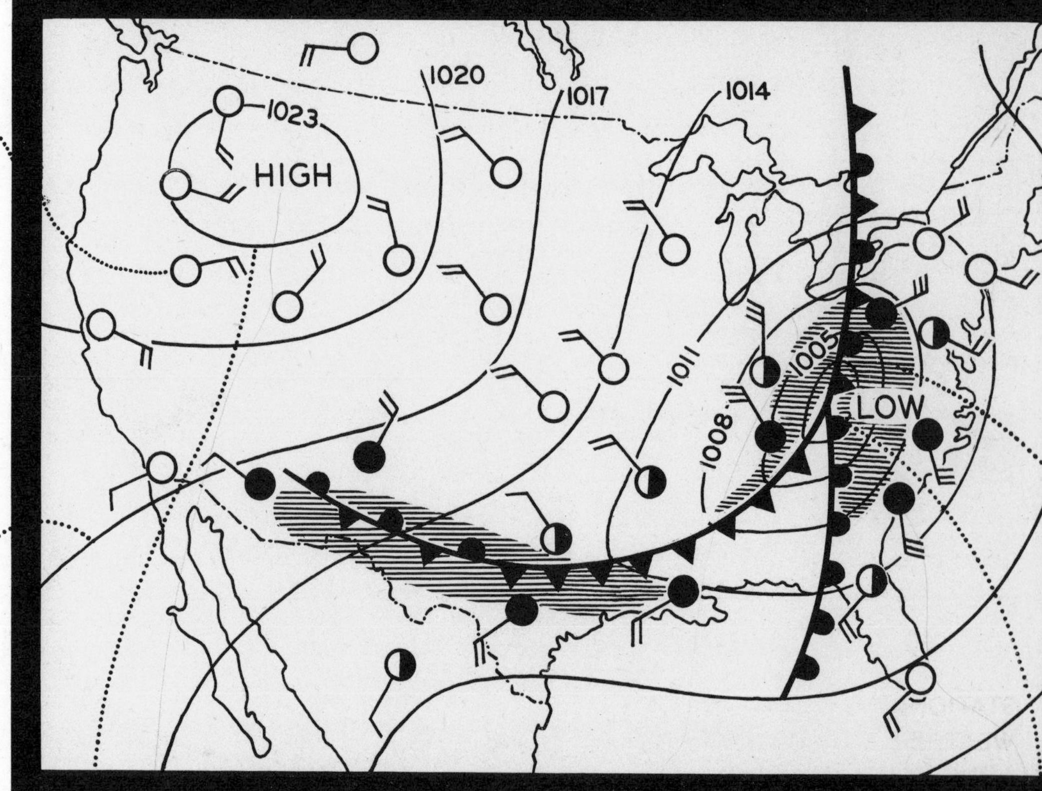

OVERCAST SYMBOLS

CLEAR

HALF CLOUDED

100% OVERCAST

OBSCURED

TEMPERATURE IS INDICATED BY A NUMBER AT UPPER LEFT STATION SYMBOL:

40

4 ISOBARS: LINES DRAWN THROUGH POINTS OF EQUAL BAROMETRIC PRESSURES. NATURALLY, WINDS BLOW FROM HIGH TO LOW.

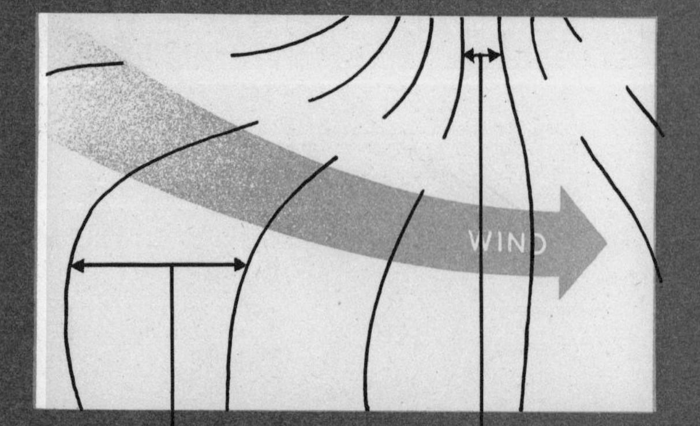

ISOBARS FAR APART MEAN MILD WINDS.

ISOBARS CLOSE MEAN FAST WINDS.

5

6

HIGH: REGION OF COLD·CLEAR·HEAVY AIR WHICH GIVES HIGH BAROMETRIC READING.

LOW: REGION OF WARM·HAZY·LIGHT AIR, STORM, RAIN. READING IS LOWER.

SOME BAROMETERS READ 1023 (MILLIBARS). SOME READ 30.21 (INCHES OF MERCURY).

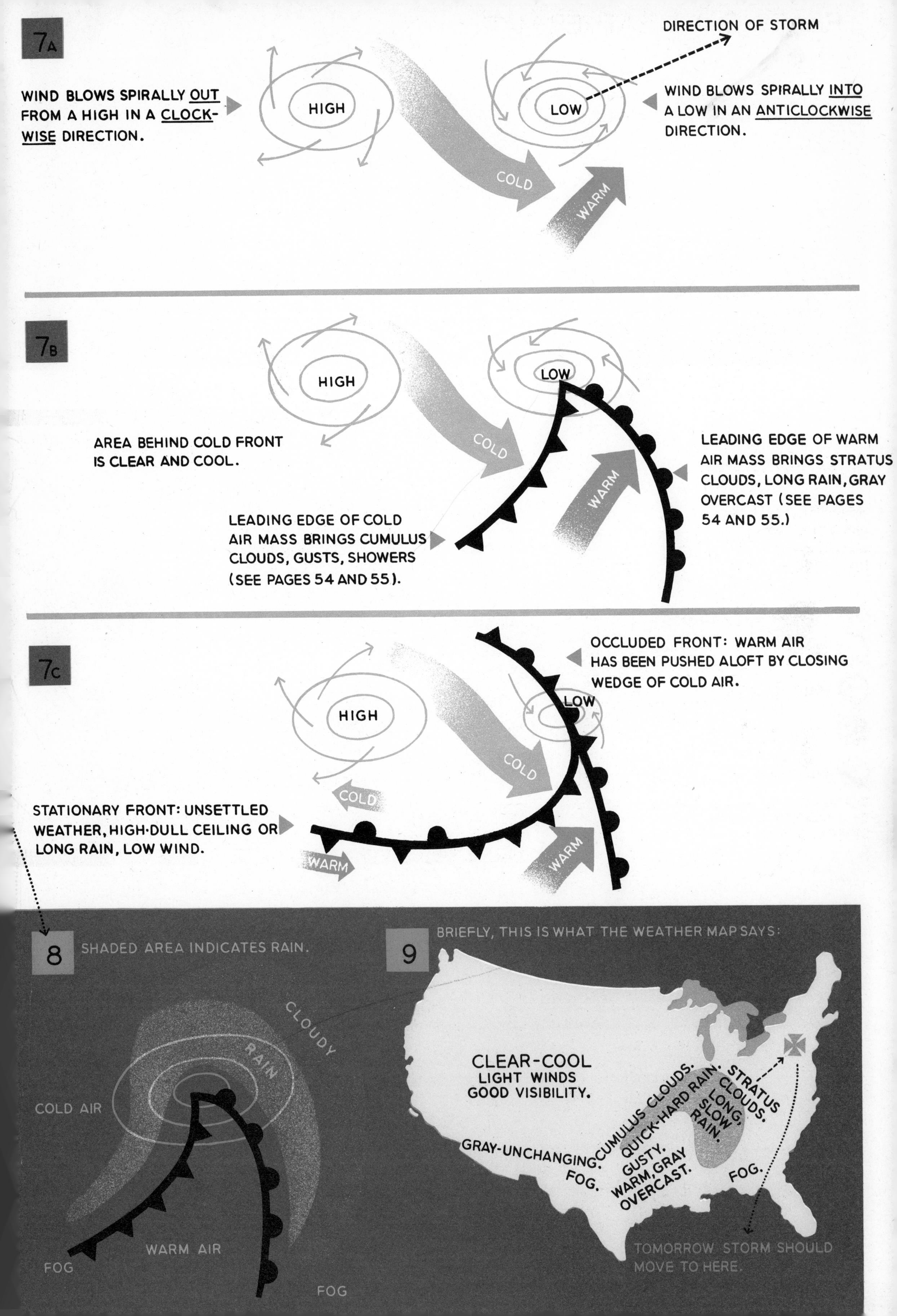
7A
WIND BLOWS SPIRALLY OUT FROM A HIGH IN A CLOCKWISE DIRECTION.
HIGH
LOW
DIRECTION OF STORM
WIND BLOWS SPIRALLY INTO A LOW IN AN ANTICLOCKWISE DIRECTION.
COLD
WARM
7B
HIGH
LOW
AREA BEHIND COLD FRONT IS CLEAR AND COOL.
COLD
WARM
LEADING EDGE OF WARM AIR MASS BRINGS STRATUS CLOUDS, LONG RAIN, GRAY OVERCAST (SEE PAGES 54 AND 55.)
LEADING EDGE OF COLD AIR MASS BRINGS CUMULUS CLOUDS, GUSTS, SHOWERS (SEE PAGES 54 AND 55).
7C
OCCLUDED FRONT: WARM AIR HAS BEEN PUSHED ALOFT BY CLOSING WEDGE OF COLD AIR.
HIGH
LOW
COLD
COLD
STATIONARY FRONT: UNSETTLED WEATHER, HIGH-DULL CEILING OR LONG RAIN, LOW WIND.
WARM
WARM
8
SHADED AREA INDICATES RAIN.
CLOUDY
RAIN
COLD AIR
WARM AIR
FOG
FOG
9
BRIEFLY, THIS IS WHAT THE WEATHER MAP SAYS:
CLEAR-COOL
LIGHT WINDS
GOOD VISIBILITY.
GRAY-UNCHANGING.
FOG.
CUMULUS CLOUDS.
QUICK-HARD RAIN.
GUSTY.
WARM, GRAY
OVERCAST.
STRATUS
CLOUDS.
LONG,
SLOW
RAIN.
FOG.
TOMORROW STORM SHOULD MOVE TO HERE.

exploring the weather

In 1946 a young General Electric scientist named Vincent J. Schaefer made history by proving a theory: he felt that if nature can make it snow, then man also should be able to make it snow. For several weeks Schaefer had little luck with his experiments, but on July twelfth he happily announced, "Now I can make it snow any time I like."

Schaefer made his snowstorm in a deep-freeze box like those you see in supermarkets. By leaning over the box and breathing into it Schaefer had created a cloud, the same kind you make in the winter when you breathe into the cold air. Next he lowered a chunk of dry ice into the box and was thrilled when snow began falling from his cloud. He later found that even a small pinch of dry ice would produce snow. This experiment told Schaefer that the water vapor in a cloud will crystallize into snow if the cloud's temperature is low enough, about 38° below zero.

Schaefer's next step was to try his experiment on a real cloud. With the help of another General Electric scientist, Nobel Prize-winning Irving Langmuir, on November thirteenth Schaefer found the kind of cloud he was looking for. He flew over it and sprayed it with flakes of dry ice. Langmuir, who was watching from the ground, was overjoyed when he saw snow falling from the cloud. When Schaefer's friends tending the weather station atop Mount Washington learned of the snow maker's success they tried their luck. By waving pieces of dry ice in the supercooled clouds that flow over the mountain they, too, discovered that they could make it snow.

Schaefer's and Langmuir's work gave positive proof that with the right kinds of clouds and with the proper conditions man can make it snow, and rain, by "cloud seeding."

Meteorologists have also used silver-iodide crystals to coax moisture from the clouds. Smoke rising from coke burners on the ground carries the crystals into the clouds above. Water vapor in the clouds condenses around the crystals and falls as rain. But again, rain making also requires that conditions be just right. For example, the cloud chosen for seeding should be supercooled to about 23°, should be a growing cloud, and should be around 4000 or 6000 feet above the ground. There are many people who can't understand why cloud seeding is such a ticklish job. In their minds if there is the slightest trace of a cloud in the sky, a cloud seeder should be able to squeeze rain from it. Some people in states having a meager rainfall are afraid that cloud seeders in neighboring states will sap all of the rain for themselves. New Mexico's Senator Clinton Anderson said that if cloud seeding is ever carried out on a grand scale, ". . . we are going to need policemen in the skies to see that some state doesn't steal another's weather."

Some meteorologists are looking ahead to the days when we launch space stations circling our planet. When this day arrives the science of meteorology may come of age in grand style. A weather patrol of mechanical meteorologists circling the earth from a distance of 4000 miles will have a bird's-eye view of the world's weather. Harry Wexler, one of our leading weather scientists, has described how a meteorological space station could locate, identify, and track storm areas from space. If such a patrol were high over Amarillo, Texas, here is some typical weather it might observe:

1. A family of three storms developing in the area from Hudson Bay to Texas. 2. A fully developed hurricane in the area of the West Indies. 3. A line of squalls in the eastern United States moving ahead of a cold front and surrounded by cumulus clouds. 4. Scattered cumulus clouds forming above heated land areas, especially over the mountains where the air rises sharply. 5. Low stratus clouds and fog off the southern California coasts, over the Great Lakes and Newfoundland, formed by warm moist air flowing over cooler surfaces.

Aided by electronic equipment, a satellite weather patrol would have a much better idea of the large-scale weather picture than earth-bound weathermen who must depend on scattered observations made close to the ground. In time our weather scientists may be able to predict the daily weather with greater accuracy. And long-range forecasts, which are now still on the experimental level, will one day benefit man in several ways. Construction companies building large dams and highways will be told how late into the fall season they can pour concrete. And people who depend on certain weather for their livelihood, owners of ski resorts and farmers, for example, might be told how to plan their season's activities with greater care.

The science of meteorology is still young. Ernest J. Christie, of the U. S. Weather Bureau in New York City, says that the weatherman and doctor have much in common. The doctor still has a long way to go in learning more about the causes and cures of disease. The weatherman also has a long way to go in learning more about the causes and prediction of weather. "The reason I say this," explains Mr. Christie, "is that many people are inclined to expect perfection from a weather forecaster without realizing that there can be no such thing."

Gradually, our meteorologists are exploring the mysterious regions of the atmosphere. They are also discovering wider uses of radar and other developments of science. For example, with the "radarscope" the weatherman can track and analyze storms far better than the human eye can. Also rockets and balloons radio to earth information about air currents and temperatures aloft. These recent developments, and others, make the weatherman's job of forecasting easier and more accurate. As our meteorologists continue to learn more about the weather they will find ways to make it serve man's needs.

index

other books about the weather

All About The Weather. Tannehill, Ivan Ray. Random House, 1953.

Book Of Storms, The. Sloane, Eric. Duell, Sloan & Pearce, Inc. 1956.

Everyday Weather And How It Works. Schneider, Herman. Whittlesey House, McGraw-Hill Book Company, 1951.

First Book Of Weather. Wyler, Rose. Franklin Watts, Inc., 1956.

How About The Weather? Fisher, Robert M. Harper & Brothers, 1951.

Hurricane Hunters. Tannehill, Ivan Ray. Dodd, Mead & Company, 1955.

Our Changing Weather. Fenton, C. L. and M. A. Doubleday & Company, Inc., 1954.

Storm. Stewart, George. Random House, Inc., 1941. (An excellent novel.)

Sun, Sea and Sky. Krick, Irving P. and Fleming, Roscoe. J. B. Lippincott Company, 1954.

Understanding The Weather. Longstreth, Thomas M. The Macmillan Company, 1953.

Weather For A Hobby. Yates, Raymond. Dodd, Mead & Company, 1956.

Weather And The Ocean Of Air. Wenstrom, William. Houghton, Mifflin Company, 1942.

Weathercasting. Laird, C. and R. Prentice-Hall, Inc., 1955.

Weathercraft. Spilhaus, Athelstan F. The Viking Press, Inc., 1951.